Great Beginnings, Grand Finales

A Midwestern Collection of Appetizers and Desserts

The Junior League of South Bend, Inc.

The Junior League of South Bend, Inc., is an organization of women committed to promoting voluntarism and to improving the community through the effective action and leadership of trained volunteers. Its purpose is exclusively educational and charitable.

The proceeds from the sale of **Great Beginnings, Grand Finales** will be returned to the community through the future projects of the Junior League of South Bend, Inc.

The recipes found in **Great Beginnings, Grand Finales** are family or restaurant favorites which have been donated by the contributors listed at the back of this book.

Additional copies of **Great Beginnings, Grand Finales** or our first cookbook **Nutbread and Nostalgia** may be obtained by using the order form in the back of the book or by calling or writing:

The Junior League of South Bend, Inc.
P.O. Box 1452
South Bend, IN 46624
219/258-6071

First Printing   10,000 copies   1991
Second Printing   10,000 copies   1993

ISBN 0-9607120-1-1

Library of Congress Catalog Card Number 91-61054

Printed in the USA

Great Beginnings, Grand Finales evolved over a period of three years, 1988 to 1991. Listed are those who served on the cookbook committee.

Committee Chairmen

Chairman	Kathy Seidl
Marketing Chairman	Nancy Wasson
Recipe Chairman	Patti Kuroski
Recorder	Kathy Abbott
Recorder	Laura Flynn
Technical Chairman	Jan Lutz
Assistant Technical Chairman	Kathi Benedix
Testing Chairman	Debbie Luther
Assistant Testing Chairman	Becky Freehauf
Treasurer	Jennifer Osthimer

Committee Members

Lona Bradford	Karen Kroft
Pat Cavanaugh	Judy Lentych
Angie Dennig	Kathy Marshall
Shelley Donnell	Gay McCrea
Jane Emanoil	Stephanie Schurz
Julie Englert	Jeanette Simon
Kari Frankenberg	Diana Skogsbergh
Chris Forry	Sandra Stone
Shirley Hamilton	Candice Stoner
Monica Hoban	

Our cover was designed by Jack Appleton, a South Bend, Indiana, artist. Jack is a graduate of the American Academy of Art in Chicago. His paintings are in many private collections, public buildings and offices. He was selected as one of Indiana's outstanding artists by the Indiana State Museum. His scenes of the University of Notre Dame and its buildings are popular on and off campus.

His work is often seen on the "Artists of America" calendar and his paintings are produced as greeting cards by Pictura of Sweden for world-wide distribution. House portraits are another specialty.

A special thank you to our exceptional photographers:

Bourdon & Bourdon Studios,
Harlan Bourdon

DeGroff Custom Photography
David Cook

Larry Gard Photography, Inc.
Larry Gard and Mark Kelly

Introduction

"Community cookbooks have long held an important place in the annals of American cookery. They reflect the true regional cuisine of a given area with great accuracy and help illuminate the social history of a period and an area as well. Historically, they have always been, and will continue to be, significant glimpses of culinary development.

But in addition to all of those rather lofty reasons, the most immediate and popular reason they have flourished is because most community cookbooks are filled with absolutely enticing recipes that you do not find in commercially printed works. **Great Beginnings, Grand Finales** is a collection of irresistible appetizers and desserts, gleaned from a part of the country known for its fine indigenous foods and clever cooks. Well-written and handsomely illustrated, this group of recipes will be popular with the most discriminating cookbook collector as well as the person who needs recipes for both family fare and entertaining."

—Marcia Adams
author of **Cooking from Quilt Country**

The spirit of Midwestern living is alive in **Great Beginnings, Grand Finales**, our fabulous collection of appetizers and desserts for all occasions. Where people gather, so does food. Within these pages you will find the perfect recipe to complement any gathering whether it is a family reunion, sporting event or elegant afternoon tea.

Our specialty cookbook offers a complete range of appetizers and desserts to be used for more than just the start or finish of a meal. Appetizers make delightful light suppers, and desserts add variety to Sunday brunch. Picnics become more fun with an assorted menu to sample. Sweets are the final grace note following an outdoor concert in the park.

The photographs in the center of the book reflect the essence of Midwestern hospitality. Any excuse to gather with friends or family and share good times and good food is an occasion to use **Great Beginnings, Grand Finales**.

Our membership and the community have enthusiastically shared with us their favorite recipes and traditions. We have carefully selected the finest of these recipes, just as we did with our first cookbook, **Nutbread and Nostalgia**. Local celebrities and restaurants have also contributed their favorites. We hope these will soon become your favorites, too.

Causes

The Junior League of South Bend, Inc., organized in 1927 as the Reserve League, began with 14 members. It became a member of the Association of Junior Leagues in 1944. Today, its membership numbers nearly 550.

The history of the Junior League of South Bend, Inc. has been one of commitment and community improvement through the effective action and leadership of trained volunteers. Members volunteer more than 10,000 hours per year and save local agencies over $100,000 annually in personnel-related costs.

A very important part of the Junior League of South Bend, Inc.'s history has been its fundraising. From the first fundraiser in 1928, a rental library, until today, the Junior League of South Bend has raised money to support its many projects. Funds raised are returned to the community. During the past decade, the Junior League of South Bend supported community projects with grants of more than $340,000 to more than 45 different projects.

The Junior League of South Bend, Inc. initiates projects in response to community needs or assists current community programs of special interest to members. Projects are supported with financial, administrative and volunteer aid. Some of our projects, past and present include:

Advocacy Center - Provides a service for people who are in financial emergency situations.

Art Market - Provides a showplace for regional artists as well as rental and purchase opportunities for the community.

CANCO - Volunteers work for the prevention of child abuse.

Center for the Homeless - Volunteers work in the family program, women's support group, and dinner service. Junior League of South Bend donated funds to build the kitchen for the Center.

Children's Museum - Volunteers are researching and developing a plan for a children's wing of the new historical museum.

Elkhart Women's Shelter - Provides a residence for battered women and their children.

Healthy Babies - Works to reduce the infant mortality rate and the number of low birth-weight babies.

Hospice (Elkhart and St. Joseph Counties) - Provides care for the terminally ill.

I'm Thumbody - A self-esteem program for elementary school children.

International Special Olympics - Responsible for the Parent Center in 1986 and 1987.

Sunday's Child - Finds permanent homes for many special-needs children.

Women's Fest - A festival celebrating women and their accomplishments.

The proceeds of ***Great Beginnings, Grand Finales*** will aid the success of our future projects.

Table of Contents

Appetizers

Desserts

Appetizers

Hot Bubble Cheese Dip

So easy, so cheesy!

Preparation: *10 minutes*
Baking: *20-30 minutes*
Yield: *4 cups*

**1 pound Cheddar cheese,
    shredded**
1 cup mayonnaise
**1½ medium onions, finely
    chopped**
**2-3 green onions, chopped,
    for garnish**

- Preheat oven to 350°.
- Combine cheese, mayonnaise and onions, and mix well.
- Place in baking dish and sprinkle with green onions.
- Bake 20-30 minutes, until hot and bubbly.
- Serve with crackers.

Ham and Brie in a Bread Bowl

Best if served on warming tray.

Preparation: *30 minutes*
Baking: *15 minutes*
Yield: *8-10 servings*

**1 (1 pound) loaf round dark
    rye or wheat bread,
    unsliced**
1 pound Brie cheese
8 ounces cooked ham, diced
**2 tablespoons chopped
    parsley**

- Preheat oven to 350°.
- Hollow out loaf of bread, leaving about a 1-inch shell.
- Cube removed bread into bite-size pieces for dipping.
- Place shell and bread cubes on cookie sheet and bake 15 minutes.
- Cut cheese into 1-inch cubes and place with ham in pan over medium-low heat.
- Cook, stirring constantly, until cheese is smooth.
- Add parsley.
- Pour mixture into bread shell.
- Serve warm with cubed bread.

Joe Kernan's Chili

Courtesy of Joe Kernan, Mayor of South Bend, Indiana.

Preparation: 45 minutes plus simmering time
Yield: 8 quarts

3 pounds ground beef
2 (30 ounce) cans red kidney beans
1 cup chopped green peppers
3 cups chopped onion
1 (7½ ounce) can jalapeño peppers, drained and chopped
2 (28 ounce) cans whole tomatoes
2 (15 ounce) cans tomato sauce
2 (12 ounce) cans tomato paste
4 cups water
1 tablespoon black pepper
1 tablespoon salt
¼ cup sugar

- Brown ground beef; drain well.
- Mash kidney beans by hand only until there are no whole beans left.
- Combine all ingredients in a covered pot.
- Simmer over low heat 2-3 hours, stirring occasionally.
- Can be served as a hearty dip with tortilla chips.

Hot Cheese and Beef Dip

Feeds the multitudes!

Preparation: 15 minutes
Cooking: 7-9 hours
Yield: 8 cups

1 pound ground beef
2 pounds pasteurized process cheese, cubed
2 medium yellow onions, chopped
3-5 jalapeño peppers, chopped
2 large tomatoes, chopped

- Brown ground beef lightly in medium skillet; drain well.
- Combine all ingredients in crock pot.
- Heat on low for 7-9 hours, stirring often.
- Serve with large size corn chips.

9

Hot Broccoli Dip

A great way to get your kids to eat their vegetables!

1 (1 pound) rye bread loaf
2 tablespoons butter
½ cup finely chopped celery
½ cup finely chopped onion
1 pound pasteurized process cheese, cubed
1 (10 ounce) package frozen chopped broccoli, thawed and drained
¼ teaspoon dried rosemary leaves, crushed

Preparation: 20 minutes
Yield: 3 cups

- Cut slice from top of bread; remove center, leaving a 1-inch shell.
- Cut removed bread into bite-size pieces.
- Melt butter in large skillet; sauté celery and onions until tender.
- Add cheese and stir over low heat until cheese is melted.
- Stir in remaining ingredients. Heat thoroughly, stirring constantly.
- Spoon into bread loaf shell and serve warm with fresh vegetables and bread cubes.

Spicy Broccoli Dip

Has lots of zip!

2 tablespoons butter or margarine
½ cup chopped onion
1 cup finely chopped celery
1 (10¾ ounce) can cream of mushroom soup
1 (4 ounce) can mushrooms, drained
8 ounces garlic cheese
8 ounces hot pepper cheese
1 (10 ounce) package frozen chopped broccoli, thawed and drained

Preparation: 30 minutes
Yield: 5-6 cups

- Melt butter in large skillet; sauté onions and celery in butter until tender.
- Add soup, mushrooms, and cheeses; stir to blend.
- When cheese is melted, add broccoli.
- Serve warm with crackers.

Hot Artichoke Spread

Can be frozen but best fresh.

Preparation: 15 minutes
Baking: 30 minutes
Yield: 2½ cups

1 (14 ounce) can artichoke hearts, drained
1 (4 ounce) can green chiles, rinsed, seeded and chopped
1 cup mayonnaise
1 cup grated Parmesan cheese

- Preheat oven to 300°.
- Remove any spikes or tough leaves from artichoke hearts.
- Chop artichoke hearts.
- Add remaining ingredients and mix well.
- Place in decorative baking dish, and bake 30 minutes.
- Serve warm with tortilla chips or crackers.

Variation: 8 ounces shredded Monterey Jack or Cheddar cheese or 4 ounces mozzarella cheese may be added for a delicious change.

Clam Dip

Quick and easy.

Preparation: 10 minutes
Baking: 30 minutes
Yield: 2 cups

12 ounces cream cheese, softened
1 (6½ ounce) can minced clams, drained (reserving juice)
8 drops hot pepper sauce
5 medium green onions, chopped
2 teaspoons lemon juice

- Preheat oven to 350°.
- Mix all ingredients thoroughly.
- Add enough reserved clam juice to bring to a spreadable consistency.
- Place in decorative baking dish, cover and bake 30 minutes.
- Serve with crackers.

Hot Crab Cocktail Spread

This is so easy and everyone loves it!

Preparation: 15 minutes
Baking: 15 minutes
Yield: 2 cups

8 ounces cream cheese, softened
1 tablespoon milk
2 teaspoons Worcestershire sauce
1 (6 ounce) can crabmeat, drained and flaked
2 tablespoons chopped green onion
2 tablespoons slivered almonds

- Preheat oven to 350°.
- Thoroughly mix cream cheese, milk, and Worcestershire sauce.
- Add crabmeat and green onions; mix.
- Turn into greased 8-inch pie plate; top with almonds.
- Bake 15 minutes or until heated through.
- Serve warm with crackers or chips.
- May be made the day before.

Sherried Crab Dip

The mustard-sherry combination is the key to its great flavor.

Preparation: 10 minutes
Yield: 3 cups

8 ounces cream cheese, softened
¼ cup evaporated milk
1½ cups crabmeat, fresh or canned (well-drained)
3 tablespoons dry sherry
1 teaspoon prepared mustard
½ teaspoon garlic powder

- In 1-quart saucepan, heat cream cheese and milk until smooth.
- Stir in remaining ingredients.
- Cook over low heat until steaming, stirring often. Do not boil.
- Serve warm with crackers or potato chips.

Chicken Pastry Slices

Your guests will appreciate your extra effort.

Preparation: 2½ hours plus chilling
Baking: 25-30 minutes
Freezes well before baking
Yield: 4-5 dozen slices

Dough
8 ounces cream cheese, softened
1 cup butter or margarine, softened
2¼ cups flour
1 teaspoon salt
¼ teaspoon mixed herbs

- Beat cream cheese and butter until smooth.
- Mix flour, salt and herbs; gradually add to cream cheese mixture.
- When dough holds together, form into ball, wrap in wax paper and refrigerate overnight.

Filling
1 small onion, minced
¼ cup butter
2 cups minced cooked chicken or turkey
½ cup minced fresh parsley
3 tablespoons minced celery
1 egg, slightly beaten
½ teaspoon salt
¼ teaspoon poultry seasoning

- Sauté onion in butter until tender, but not brown.
- Stir in remaining ingredients and mix well.

To assemble:
- Allow pastry to set at room temperature for 30 minutes.
- Cut into fourths; work with one portion at a time.
- Roll out on floured board to a rectangle, 4x18x⅛-inch.
- Place ¼ of filling in center of strip.
- Draw up edges to meet and pinch together to seal. Moisten with a little water to help it hold together.
- Transfer filled strip to ungreased baking sheet.
- Repeat process with other three portions of dough.
- Chill 1-2 hours.
- Preheat oven to 325°.
- Cut rolls into 1-inch slices, separating slices slightly.
- Brush lightly with a beaten egg mixed with 1 teaspoon water.
- Bake 25-30 minutes or until lightly browned.

Chicken Fingers with Plum Sauce

A new taste for your next party.

Preparation: 45 minutes plus overnight marinating
Baking: 35-40 minutes
Freezes well after baking
Yield: 12-14 appetizer servings

Chicken Fingers
6 whole chicken breasts, boned

- Cut chicken into ½-inch strips.

Marinade
1½ cups buttermilk
2 tablespoons lemon juice
2 teaspoons Worcestershire sauce
1 teaspoon soy sauce
1 teaspoon paprika
1 tablespoon Greek seasoning (dillweed, rosemary, basil and thyme)
1 teaspoon salt
1 teaspoon pepper
2 garlic cloves, minced

- Combine marinade ingredients.
- Add chicken, mixing until well-coated.
- Cover and refrigerate overnight.

Breading
4 cups soft bread crumbs
½ cup sesame seeds
¼ cup butter or margarine, melted
¼ cup shortening, melted

- Preheat oven to 350°.
- Drain chicken thoroughly.
- Combine bread crumbs and sesame seeds, mixing well.
- Add chicken and toss to coat.
- Place chicken in 2 greased 9x13-inch baking pans.
- Combine butter and shortening; brush on chicken.
- Bake 35-40 minutes.
- Serve warm with Plum Sauce.

Plum Sauce
1½ cups red plum jam
1½ tablespoons prepared mustard
1½ tablespoons prepared horseradish
1½ teaspoons lemon juice

- Combine all ingredients in small saucepan, mixing well.
- Place over low heat just until warm, stirring constantly.
- Serve as dipping sauce with chicken fingers.

Oriental Chicken Wings

Great taste—worth the messy fingers!

Preparation: 20 minutes
Baking: 50 minutes
Yield: 36 appetizers

3 pounds chicken wings
⅓ cup soy sauce
2 tablespoons vegetable oil
2 tablespoons chili sauce
½ cup honey
1 teaspoon salt
½ teaspoon fresh grated ginger
¼ teaspoon garlic powder
¼ teaspoon cayenne pepper, optional

- Wash chicken wings and pat dry.
- Remove and discard tips. Separate remaining wing into 2 pieces and place in airtight container.
- Mix remaining ingredients and pour over chicken wings.
- Cover and refrigerate overnight, turning occasionally.
- Preheat oven to 375°.
- Place chicken wings on foil-lined broiler pan.
- Brush with marinade and bake 25 minutes.
- Turn chicken wings, brush with marinade and bake 25 minutes longer.

Parmesan Chicken Wings

May be made a day ahead and reheated.

Preparation: 45 minutes
Baking: 1 hour
Yield: 60 appetizers

2 cups grated Parmesan cheese
2 teaspoons dried oregano
1 tablespoon dried parsley
1 teaspoon paprika
1 teaspoon salt
1 teaspoon freshly ground pepper
30 whole chicken wings
1 cup melted butter

- Preheat oven to 350°.
- Line jelly roll pan with aluminum foil to make clean-up easy.
- Mix all dry ingredients together in bowl.
- Remove and discard wing tips. Separate remaining wing into two pieces.
- Dip wings in melted butter.
- Roll in dry ingredients.
- Place in pan in single layer.
- Bake 1 hour.

Almond Chicken Puffs

Special spicy flavor.

Preparation: 1 hours
Baking: 10-15 minutes
Freezes well after baking
Yield: 48 puffs

1 cup flour
1 cup chicken stock
2 teaspoons seasoned salt
¼ teaspoon cayenne pepper
1 teaspoon celery seed
1 tablespoon dried parsley flakes
1 tablespoon Worcestershire sauce
½ cup margarine
4 eggs
½ cup finely diced cooked chicken
2 tablespoons almonds, chopped

- Sift flour.
- In a saucepan over low heat, combine chicken stock, seasoned salt, cayenne pepper, celery seed, dried parsley flakes, Worcestershire sauce and margarine; bring to a boil.
- Add flour all at once, stirring until mixture forms a ball and leaves the side of the pan, about 3 minutes.
- Remove from heat.
- Add eggs, one at a time, beating thoroughly after each addition.
- Continue beating until a thick dough is formed.
- Preheat oven to 450°.
- Stir chicken and almonds into dough.
- Drop by small teaspoonfuls onto greased baking sheet.
- Bake 10-15 minutes or until browned.
- Serve hot.
- Puffs may be frozen in an airtight container after baking. To thaw and crisp, put puffs on baking sheet and heat at 250° for 10-15 minutes.

Variation: Use with your favorite dipping sauce.

King Size Steak Bites

An appetizer with some meat to it (ha! ha!).

Preparation: 20 minutes plus marinating time
Broiling: 10 minutes
Yield: 16-20 servings

4 pounds round steak, cut 1-inch thick
seasoned meat tenderizer
1 cup red wine vinegar
1 clove garlic, crushed
½ cup butter
1 tablespoon Worcestershire sauce
½ teaspoon salt
dash of pepper
2 drops hot pepper sauce

- Apply meat tenderizer to steak as label directs.
- In a large shallow pan, mix vinegar and garlic.
- Add steak. Cover and refrigerate for 1½ hours or overnight, turning once.
- Broil steak approximately 10-12 minutes for medium rare, turning once.
- In small saucepan, melt butter over medium heat. Add Worcestershire sauce, salt, pepper, hot pepper sauce, and 2 tablespoons of steak marinade.
- Cut steak into cubes and place in chafing dish. Pour butter sauce over meat. Serve with toothpicks.

Chinese Meatballs

Chunks of pineapple and green pepper may be added for color.

Preparation: 2½ hours
Yield: 200 meatballs

Meatballs
2 (8 ounce) cans water
  chestnuts, drained and
  chopped
3 medium bunches green
  onions, chopped
2½ pounds lean ground beef
2½ pounds ground pork
¼ cup soy sauce
6 eggs, slightly beaten
1½ teaspoons salt
2½ cups bread crumbs
cornstarch
vegetable oil

- Mix together water chestnuts, green onions, and meat.
- Add soy sauce, eggs, salt, and bread crumbs. Mix thoroughly and chill.
- Form into small balls. Roll lightly in cornstarch.
- Heat vegetable oil in skillet. Brown meatballs and drain.

Sauce
1 cup vinegar
2 cups pineapple juice
¾ cup sugar
2 cups beef consommé
2 tablespoons soy sauce
3 tablespoons grated fresh
  ginger (or 5 tablespoons
  chopped crystallized
  ginger)
½ cup cornstarch
1 cup cold water

- In a medium saucepan, heat vinegar, pineapple juice, sugar, consommé, soy sauce, and ginger over medium heat.
- Combine cornstarch and water. Gradually add to vinegar mixture.
- Cook, stirring constantly, until clear and thickened.
- Add meatballs to sauce. Serve in chafing dish.

Sweet and Sour Meatballs

*Great to keep on hand in the
freezer for surprise guests.*

*Preparation: 45 minutes
Baking: 90 minutes
Freezes well after baking
Yield: 80 meatballs*

Meatballs
**2 pounds ground round
1 (1 ounce) envelope dried
   onion soup mix
1 cup bread crumbs
3 eggs**

- Mix together ground round, soup mix,
  bread crumbs and eggs.
- Form into walnut-sized balls. Place in a
  9x13-inch baking pan.

Sauce
**1 (12 ounce) bottle chili
   sauce
1½ cups water
½ cup firmly packed brown
   sugar
1 (17 ounce) can sauerkraut,
   drained
1 (17 ounce) can whole
   cranberry sauce**

- Preheat oven to 350°.
- Combine all sauce ingredients and pour
  over meatballs.
- Bake 1½ hours.
- Serve in a chafing dish or crock pot with
  toothpicks.

Chili Grape Meatballs

*What a surprising combination
of flavors!*

*Preparation: 40 minutes plus simmering
Yield: 5 dozen meatballs*

**2 pounds ground beef
4 eggs
1 teaspoon chopped fresh
   parsley
6 slices bread, crumbed
2 cups grape jam (not jelly)
1 (8 ounce) jar chili sauce**

- Combine beef, eggs, parsley and bread
  crumbs.
- Roll into ¾-inch meatballs.
- Brown in skillet.
- Combine jam and chili sauce.
- Place sauce in crock pot or electric skillet.
- Add meatballs to sauce and simmer 4
  hours.
- Serve in chafing dish.

Filet of Beef with Rosemary

Easy and impressive.

Preparation: 45 minutes
Baking: 20 minutes
Yield: 12-16 servings

3-4 pounds beef tenderloin
salt, pepper, and rosemary to
taste
2 (1 pound) loaves French
bread
Herb Butter (see below)
1 bunch watercress

- Preheat oven to 450°.
- Rub beef with salt, pepper, and rosemary.
- Insert meat thermometer in thickest part of meat.
- Bake until thermometer registers 140° for rare or 160° for medium rare, about 20-30 minutes.
- Let meat stand 20 minutes before slicing.
- Slice French bread into ½-inch diagonal slices.
- Spread one side of each slice with Herb Butter.
- Put thin slice of filet on top of each bread slice; top with watercress.

Herb Butter

1 cup butter, softened
1 teaspoon garlic powder
2 teaspoons lemon pepper
2 teaspoons parsley
1 teaspoon onion powder
1 teaspoon paprika
1 teaspoon oregano

- Combine all ingredients.
- Beat in mixer until blended.
- Makes enough for full recipe. May be cut in half for other uses.

Herbed Pork Tenderloin

Simple to prepare.

Preparation: 1 hour 15 minutes
Baking: 30 minutes
Yield: 12-15 servings

1½ pounds whole pork
tenderloin
¼ cup dry white wine
½ teaspoon marjoram leaves
½ teaspoon dried rosemary
leaves
1 garlic clove, minced
6 tablespoons butter, melted
pepper to taste
2 loaves narrow French
bread, sliced ¼-inch thick
parsley to garnish

- Place tenderloin in 8x11-inch baking pan.
- Combine wine, marjoram, rosemary, and garlic.
- Blend well and pour over meat.
- Cover and marinate at room temperature for 20 minutes.
- Preheat oven to 450°.
- Remove pork from marinade and place on baking sheet.
- Add butter to marinade.
- Roast on middle rack of oven for 30 minutes basting meat thoroughly every 10 minutes.
- Remove from oven and allow to cool to room temperature.
- Slice meat very thin.
- Assemble just before serving.
- Quickly dip each slice of bread into juices of pan, just enough to slightly moisten.
- Arrange three slices of meat on each slice of bread.
- Garnish with a tiny sprig of parsley.

Mini Reubens

Try these open-faced sandwiches for St. Patrick's Day.

Preparation: 20-30 minutes
Broiling: 5 minutes
Yield: 20 servings

20 slices party rye bread
8 ounces Dijon mustard
12 ounces shaved deli corned beef
1 (14 ounce) can sauerkraut, well drained
8 ounces baby Swiss cheese, sliced

- On a baking sheet, layer sandwiches in the following order: bread slice, mustard, corned beef, sauerkraut, and cheese slice.
- Broil until cheese melts.
- Serve warm.

Variation: Thousand Island salad dressing may be substituted for Dijon mustard.

Rigatoni Marinara with Sausage

Courtesy of Regis Philbin, a famous Notre Dame alumnus and talk show host.

Preparation: 45 minutes plus simmering time
Yield: 6-8 servings

1-2 cloves garlic, minced
1 tablespoon chopped parsley
1 tablespoon olive oil
1 (28 ounce) can peeled whole tomatoes, drained
1 (6 ounce) can tomato paste
½ teaspoon basil
1 bay leaf
1 teaspoon salt
⅛ teaspoon pepper
oregano to taste
1 pound sweet Italian link sausage
1 pound rigatoni

- In large pot, sauté garlic and parsley in oil until light brown. Do not let it burn.
- Chop tomatoes; add to garlic mixture along with tomato paste and seasonings.
- Brown sausage well in large skillet; drain.
- Add sausage to sauce; simmer at least 45 minutes.
- Cook rigatoni according to package directions; drain well.
- Place drained rigatoni on platter; cover with sauce and top with sausage links.
- Serves 4 as main course for lunch or dinner.

Ham and Eggs Creole

Courtesy of Ernestine Raclin, Chairman of the Board, First Source Bank.

Preparation: 40 minutes
Yield: 12-16 servings

6 tablespoons butter or margarine, divided
1 large onion, minced
1 large green pepper, diced
3 tablespoons flour
1 (10¾ ounce) can tomato soup
1¼ cups beef stock
½ teaspoon white pepper
⅛ teaspoon dried thyme
⅛ teaspoon hot pepper sauce
½ teaspoon Worcestershire sauce
⅛ teaspoon dried chili peppers
pinch of salt
1½ cups shredded Cheddar cheese
8 hard-boiled eggs
1½ cups diced, cooked ham
¾ cup soft bread crumbs

- Preheat oven to 350°.
- Melt 3 tablespoons butter in large, heavy skillet.
- Sauté onions and green pepper over low heat until limp and golden.
- Add flour; blend into butter until smooth.
- Pour in tomato soup and beef stock slowly, stirring until smooth.
- Bring to a slow boil, stirring constantly.
- Add white pepper, thyme, hot pepper sauce, Worcestershire sauce, chili peppers and salt; mix well.
- Add shredded cheese; continue stirring 2 minutes. Remove from heat.
- Slice hard-boiled eggs (not too thick) into greased 8-inch square baking dish; mix lightly with ham.
- Pour sauce over ham and eggs and mix.
- Sprinkle bread crumbs on top.
- Dot with remaining butter.
- Cover and refrigerate until needed.
- At serving time, preheat oven to 350°, and bake, uncovered, 15-20 minutes or until bread crumbs are nicely toasted.
- Cut into small squares and serve on a brunch buffet.
- This recipe can be doubled.

Sausage Mushroom Turnovers

Great with dipping sauce.

Preparation: 1 hour 30 minutes
Baking: 15 minutes
Freezes well before baking
Yield: 4 dozen

Pastry
½ cup butter, softened
9 ounces cream cheese,
  softened
1½ cups flour

- Cream butter and cream cheese. Gradually add flour.
- Mix until smooth.
- Cover and chill.

Filling
½ pound mushrooms,
  chopped
1 onion, chopped
3 tablespoons butter
½ pound bulk sausage,
  browned and drained
½ teaspoon salt
pepper to taste
2 tablespoons flour
¼ cup sour cream

- Sauté mushrooms and onions in butter.
- Add sausage, salt, and pepper.
- Sprinkle mixture with flour.
- Stir in sour cream. Cook until thickened, stirring constantly. Set aside.

To Assemble:
- Preheat oven to 425°.
- Roll pastry to ⅛-inch thickness on floured wax paper.
- Cut into circles with 3-inch glass or round cookie cutter.
- Drop 1 teaspoon filling onto each circle.
- Fold in half and press edges together with a fork.
- Prick tops with fork.
- Bake 15 minutes. Serve warm.

Shrimp Delights

Shrimply delightful!

Preparation: 20 minutes plus freezing
Broiling: 5 minutes
Yield: 48 appetizers

**6 tablespoons margarine,
  softened**
**1 (5 ounce) jar sharp
  pasteurized process cheese
  spread**
2 tablespoons mayonnaise
¼ teaspoon seasoned salt
¼ teaspoon garlic salt
**2 (4½ ounce) cans shrimp,
  rinsed and drained**
12 English muffin halves
paprika

- Place margarine, cheese spread, mayonnaise and seasonings in a mixing bowl.
- Blend with electric mixer.
- Mash shrimp and add to mixture.
- Mix until well blended.
- Spread muffin halves with mixture.
- Freeze at least 10 minutes; cut each half into 4 pieces.
- Broil 5 minutes or until bubbly and crisp.
- Sprinkle with paprika. Serve warm.

*Variation: 1 (7 ounce) can crabmeat, drained,
may be substituted for the shrimp.*

Shrimp Canapés

*Freeze ahead for busy holiday
season.*

Preparation: 15 minutes
Baking: 8-10 minutes
Freezes well before baking
Yield: 3 dozen canapés

**1 (4½ ounce) can shrimp,
  drained**
**1¼ cups shredded Swiss
  cheese**
½ cup mayonnaise
¼ teaspoon curry powder
1 teaspoon lemon juice
1 tablespoon minced onion
salt and pepper to taste
melba crackers

- Preheat oven to 350°.
- Place shrimp, cheese, mayonnaise, curry powder, lemon juice, onion, salt and pepper in a mixing bowl.
- Mix until well blended.
- Spread mixture on crackers.
- Bake 8-10 minutes or until cheese melts.
- Serve warm.

Crab Wontons

Try these with Pat's Mustard Sauce, page 41.

Preparation: 1 hour
Yield: 50-55 appetizers

1 pound cream cheese, room temperature
1 pound crabmeat
1 tablespoon chopped garlic
⅛ teaspoon Worcestershire sauce
3 drops hot pepper sauce
1 teaspoon salt
1 teaspoon pepper
¼ cup grated Parmesan cheese
1 package wonton wrappers (50-55 wrappers)

- Combine all ingredients except wrappers and mix well.
- While preparing wontons, keep unused wrappers covered with a damp towel or plastic wrap so they will not dry out.
- Place 1 teaspoon filling in each wrapper; fold corners together in center and pinch to seal.
- Deep fry wontons in hot vegetable oil for 30 seconds, turning occasionally to promote even browning.
- To reheat, bake in oven for 5 minutes at 425°.

Crab Rolls

Must be frozen before baking.

Preparation: 30 minutes
Baking: 15 minutes
Yield: 60-80 rolls

8 ounces pasteurized process cheese
2 cups butter, divided
2 (6 ounce) cans crabmeat, drained
20 slices white bread
1 (2⅜ ounce) box sesame seeds, lightly toasted

- In a small saucepan, melt cheese and 1 cup butter. Remove from heat and cool.
- Stir in crabmeat.
- Trim crusts from bread.
- Flatten each slice with rolling pin.
- Spread crabmeat mixture on bread and roll up.
- Melt remaining 1 cup butter and brush on rolls.
- Sprinkle sesame seeds on rolls.
- Place on baking sheet and freeze.
- Preheat oven to 400°.
- Cut each roll into thirds or fourths.
- Bake 15 minutes.

King Crab Canapés

Can be made in larger muffin tins and served for a ladies' luncheon.

Preparation: 30 minutes
Baking: 15-20 minutes
Freezes well after baking
Yield: 2 dozen canapés

1 (8 ounce) package refrigerated butterflake biscuits
6 ounces cream cheese
6 ounces king crabmeat, rinsed, drained and picked clean
2 tablespoons mayonnaise
2 tablespoons grated Parmesan cheese
½ cup shredded Cheddar cheese
2 tablespoons minced shallots
1 teaspoon Worcestershire sauce
seasoned salt to taste
paprika

- Preheat oven to 375°.
- Separate dinner rolls into 3 layers. Place in ungreased mini-muffin tins.
- Combine cream cheese, crabmeat, mayonnaise, cheeses, shallots, Worcestershire sauce and seasoned salt in a mixing bowl; mix well.
- Place mixture into cups.
- Sprinkle with paprika.
- Bake 15-20 minutes or until lightly browned.
- Cool 5 minutes before serving.

Cheesy Crab Crêpes

Impress your guests. Well worth the time.

Preparation: 2 hours
Baking: 10-12 minutes
Yield: 3-4 dozen

Crêpes
1 cup flour
1½ cups milk
2 eggs
1 tablespoon vegetable oil
¼ teaspoon salt

- Combine all ingredients in a mixing bowl.
- Beat with a rotary beater until blended.
- Heat crêpe pan or 6-inch skillet.
- Remove pan from heat and spoon in 2 tablespoons of batter.
- Lift and tilt skillet to spread batter evenly.
- Return pan to heat and lightly brown one side only.
- Remove crêpe from pan.
- Repeat with remainder of batter.
- Using a 2½-inch round cookie cutter, cut 3 circles from each crêpe.
- Carefully fit circles into greased 1¾-inch muffin pans.

Crab Filling
1 (7½ ounce) can crabmeat, drained
1 cup shredded Swiss cheese
¼ cup chopped water chestnuts
½ cup mayonnaise
1 tablespoon chopped green onion
1 teaspoon lemon juice
¼ teaspoon curry powder
snipped parsley

- Preheat oven to 400°.
- Place crabmeat, cheese, water chestnuts, mayonnaise, onion, lemon juice and curry powder in a mixing bowl. Mix until well combined.
- Spoon rounded teaspoon of filling into each cup.
- Bake 10-12 minutes.
- Sprinkle with parsley; serve warm.

Spinach Crab Balls

*Try these with Pat's Mustard
Sauce, page 41.*

*Preparation: 30 minutes
Baking: 12-15 minutes
Freezes well before baking
Yield: 3-4 dozen*

**1 tablespoon butter
1 large onion, minced
2 (10 ounce) packages frozen
    chopped spinach, thawed,
    drained and patted dry
6 eggs
2 tablespoons flour
6 slices bacon, cooked and
    crumbled
2/3 cup butter, softened
1 (7½ ounce) can crabmeat,
    drained
3 cups seasoned stuffing
¼ teaspoon pepper
½ teaspoon salt
½ teaspoon dillweed
1 clove garlic, mashed**

- Preheat oven to 325°.
- Melt butter in skillet.
- Stir in onions and sauté until tender.
- Mix thoroughly with remaining ingredients.
- Form into 1½-inch balls and place on baking sheet.
- Bake 12-15 minutes.
- Serve warm.

Sauterne Clam Puffs

*Serve warm with chilled wine or
sherry.*

*Preparation: 20 minutes
Broiling: 5 minutes
Yield: 18-20 appetizers*

**8 ounces cream cheese,
    softened
¼ cup Sauterne (or white
    wine)
2 (6½ ounce) cans minced
    clams, drained
toast rounds
4 slices bacon, cooked and
    crumbled**

- Blend cream cheese and wine.
- Add clams and mix well.
- Spread mixture on toast rounds.
- Sprinkle with bacon.
- Broil 5 minutes or until crisp. Watch carefully—these burn easily!

Seafood Strudel

For people on the go, buy your favorite seafood salad at your local deli.

Preparation: 40 minutes
Baking: 20 minutes
Yield: 10-12 servings

Seafood Salad
8 ounces crabmeat
8 ounces small shrimp
8 ounces lobster pieces
1 cup diced celery
1 green pepper, chopped
2 hard-boiled eggs, diced
¾ cup mayonnaise

- Combine all ingredients thoroughly; set aside.

Strudel
12 sheets phyllo dough,
  thawed as package directs
1 cup butter, melted
1 cup fine dry bread crumbs

- Preheat oven to 400°.
- Lightly dampen a kitchen towel.
- Place one sheet of phyllo dough on the towel.
- Brush dough with butter and sprinkle lightly with bread crumbs.
- Repeat 4 times and end with the sixth sheet of dough.
- Place half of the seafood salad on narrow edge of dough, leaving a 2-inch border on each side.
- Fold in the sides and roll up dough.
- Place roll on a buttered baking sheet.
- Brush dough with butter.
- Repeat using remaining phyllo dough and seafood salad.
- Bake 20 minutes or until dough is slightly browned.
- Slice into pieces and serve warm.

Asparagus Roll-ups

*These make an unusual
springtime side dish.*

Preparation: 45 minutes
Baking: 20 minutes
Yield: approximately 30 appetizers

**1 loaf thinly sliced white
  bread, crusts removed
about 30 thin fresh
  asparagus spears
½ cup butter, melted
grated Parmesan cheese**

- Preheat oven to 350°.
- Blanch asparagus in boiling water about 3
  minutes.
- Flatten each slice of bread with rolling pin.
- Brush a bread slice lightly with melted
  butter and sprinkle with cheese.
- Place asparagus spear at the corner of
  slice and roll up diagonally.
- Repeat until each spear is wrapped.
- Place wrapped spears on baking sheet;
  brush with butter and sprinkle with cheese.
- Bake until bread is golden, about 20
  minutes.

Artichoke Cheese Puffs

Easy finger food.

Preparation: 30 minutes
Baking: 5 minutes
Yield: 32 puffs

**8 slices whole wheat bread
⅓ cup grated Parmesan
  cheese
¾ cup mayonnaise
¼ cup minced green onion
½ teaspoon Worcestershire
  sauce
½ teaspoon white pepper
1 (14 ounce) can water-
  packed artichoke hearts,
  drained and quartered**

- Preheat oven to 400°.
- Lightly toast bread and cut each slice into
  4 rectangles.
- Combine Parmesan cheese, mayonnaise,
  green onion, Worcestershire sauce, and
  white pepper.
- Place an artichoke quarter on each bread
  rectangle.
- Spread cheese mixture on top.
- Bake in upper ⅓ of oven 5 minutes or
  until puffy.

Cucumber Cheese Rolls

Delicious!

Preparation: 1 hour
Baking: 20 minutes
Freezes well before baking
Yield: 60 servings

1 loaf thinly sliced sandwich bread
½ cup butter, melted
6 ounces cream cheese, softened
1 cup chopped cucumbers
4 green onions, chopped
2 tablespoons milk
4 teaspoons sugar
½ teaspoon salt

- Preheat oven to 400°.
- Remove crust from bread.
- Spread each slice of bread with melted butter.
- Mix remaining ingredients and spread mixture on each bread slice; roll jelly roll fashion.
- Place on buttered baking sheet.
- Brush lightly with melted butter.
- Slice each roll into 3 pieces.
- Bake 20 minutes.

Dijon Green Onion Appetizer

Guaranteed not to last!

Preparation: 15 minutes
Broiling: about 1 minute
Yield: 40 appetizers

1 cup mayonnaise
½ cup finely grated Parmesan cheese
2 generous tablespoons Dijon mustard
1 loaf French bread, cut into ½-inch slices
ripe olives, sliced
green onions, sliced

- Mix together mayonnaise, Parmesan cheese and Dijon mustard.
- Spread generous amounts on French bread slices.
- Broil until slightly browned, approximately 1 minute.
- Remove from oven and sprinkle with olives and green onions.

Hardwood Grilled Pizza with Tomatoes and Fresh Herbs

From LaSalle Hardwood Grille, South Bend, Indiana

Preparation: 1 hour plus rising time
Yield: 12 servings

Herb Oil
5 fresh basil leaves
3 fresh sage leaves
2 tablespoons fresh oregano leaves
1 medium garlic clove
¼ cup olive oil
¼ teaspoon salt

- Combine herbs and garlic in workbowl of food processor and pulse to mince.
- Mix in salt and oil.
- Can be refrigerated for 1 day.

Pizza
1 package active dry yeast
½ cup warm water (105-115°.)
1½-1¾ cups flour
1 tablespoon olive oil
½ teaspoon salt
1 medium tomato, seeded and diced
1 small onion, sliced very thin
4 ounces mozzarella cheese, thinly sliced
fresh basil leaves for garnish

- Combine yeast, water, flour, olive oil and salt and knead for 10 minutes.
- Cover with a damp cloth and let double in volume.
- Punch down dough and divide into 2 pieces.
- Roll out on floured surface into 8-inch circles.
- Brush with Herb Oil.
- Grill in a kettle grill over a hot wood fire with cover on until browned on underside.
- Remove from fire and place on foil, grilled side up.
- Spread 1 teaspoon of Herb Oil over each pizza.
- Arrange topping ingredients over each crust in this order: onions, mozzarella cheese and tomatoes.
- Return to grill; cover and cook just until bottoms are browned and cheese is melted.
- Snip fresh basil over top and serve immediately.

Crab Stuffed Mushroom Caps

*Thanks to The Matterhorn
Restaurant, Elkhart, Indiana*

*Preparation: 30 minutes
Baking: 12-15 minutes
Yield: 16 mushroom caps*

1 tablespoon butter
¼ cup finely diced onion
¼ cup finely diced celery
1 ounce white wine
1 teaspoon salt
¼ teaspoon white pepper
½ teaspoon thyme
1 teaspoon lemon juice
4 ounces king, snow or lump crabmeat
1 ounce heavy cream or half-and-half
¼ cup shredded baby Swiss cheese
½ cup bread crumbs
16 large mushrooms, stems removed
16 small thin slices baby Swiss cheese

- Preheat oven to 375°.
- Melt butter in medium skillet.
- Sauté onions and celery in butter until tender.
- Add wine, seasonings, lemon juice and crabmeat; simmer 3 minutes.
- Add cream and shredded cheese; cook until cheese melts.
- Add bread crumbs.
- Spoon crab mixture into mushroom caps.
- Top with slices of baby Swiss cheese.
- Bake 12-15 minutes or until cheese is lightly browned.

Mushroom Cheese Logs

Easily sliced with dental floss.

Preparation: 15-20 minutes
Baking: 12 minutes
Freezes well before baking
Yield: 32 appetizers

**1 (4 ounce) can mushrooms,
    drained and chopped**
**3 ounces cream cheese,
    softened**
¼ teaspoon seasoned salt
**1 (8 ounce) package
    refrigerated crescent rolls**
1 egg, beaten
poppy seeds

- Preheat oven to 375°.
- Blend mushrooms, cream cheese and salt.
- Unroll crescent dough; lay rectangles end-to-end to form one long strip. Press seams together to seal.
- Spread mushroom mixture over dough and roll up starting on long side.
- Brush with egg.
- Sprinkle with poppy seeds.
- Cut into 32 slices with dental floss. Put floss under the roll and cut through by pretending to tie the floss.
- Bake on baking sheet 12 minutes.

Mushroom Delights

Best when served warm.

Preparation: 15 minutes
Baking: 5 minutes
Freezes well before baking
Yield: 30 appetizers

1 pound mushrooms, sliced
¾ cup butter, divided
1 clove garlic, minced
**minced fresh or dry parsley
    for color**
1 package party rye bread
**¼ cup grated Parmesan
    cheese**

- Preheat oven to 350°.
- Melt ¼ cup butter; lightly sauté sliced mushrooms. Drain well.
- Soften remaining ½ cup butter; add garlic and parsley.
- Spread bread slices with butter mixture.
- Spread mushrooms evenly on bread slices.
- Sprinkle with Parmesan cheese.
- Place on baking sheets and bake until bread is toasted on edges, about 5 minutes.
- These may be frozen on baking sheets before baking, then stored in freezer container. To serve, place on baking sheet and bake as directed above.

Haystack Baked Stuffed Mushrooms

May be served as a first course appetizer in individual gratin dishes.

Preparation: 45 minutes
Baking: 15-20 minutes
Yield: 18 mushroom caps

18 mushrooms (about the size of a half-dollar), washed
½ small onion
2 garlic cloves
3 tablespoons vegetable oil
3 tablespoons butter
¼ cup sliced almonds, toasted
1½ teaspoons dried parsley flakes
1½ teaspoons Worcestershire sauce
½ teaspoon dried basil
½ teaspoon paprika
4-6 tablespoons dry sherry
4-6 tablespoons bread crumbs
freshly grated Parmesan cheese
butter
freshly ground pepper

- Remove stems from mushrooms and set caps aside.
- Combine stems, onion and garlic in workbowl of food processor; process until finely chopped.
- Heat half of vegetable oil and butter in small saucepan.
- Add mushroom mixture and sauté over medium-high heat for 4-5 minutes, adding more vegetable oil and butter if needed.
- Add almonds, parsley, Worcestershire sauce, basil, paprika and sherry. Bring to a simmer.
- Remove from heat and add bread crumbs. Toss lightly.
- Preheat oven to 400°.
- Heat remaining vegetable oil and butter in saucepan and sauté mushroom caps over high heat for 1-2 minutes.
- Place caps rounded-side down in baking pan.
- Divide crumb mixture among caps.
- Dust with Parmesan cheese, dot with butter and sprinkle with pepper.
- Bake until heated through, 15-20 minutes.

Giant Ravioli with Shiitake Mushrooms and Brandy Cream Sauce

Courtesy of Carriage House Restaurant, South Bend, Indiana.

Preparation: 2 hours plus setting time
Yield: 6-8 servings

Pasta
3 eggs, room temperature
2 cups flour

- Mix eggs and flour in food processor.
- Wrap in plastic and let stand 1 hour.

Filling
¼ cup butter
2 shallots, finely chopped
1 pound shiitake mushrooms, coarsely chopped

- Melt butter in small skillet.
- Add shallots and mushrooms. Sauté until tender.
- Let mixture cool in skillet.
- Roll pasta dough into 2 very thin sheets.
- Place mushroom filling on 1 sheet by small spoonfuls.
- Cover with second sheet of dough. Cut with pastry wheel to desired size.
- May be made ahead to this point.
- Drop into boiling water. Lift out carefully when tender.

Sauce
¼ cup brandy
1 cup heavy cream
2 tablespoons butter
fresh snipped chives

- Without cleaning skillet used for mushroom mixture, deglaze pan with brandy. Brandy may flame, so be prepared!
- Add cream. Cook and stir until thick.
- Add butter. Stir until melted
- Spoon cream sauce over ravioli. Garnish with chives.

Variation: Morel mushrooms may be substituted for shiitakes in season.

Zucchini Appetizers

Delicious item for a brunch buffet.

Preparation: 15-20 minutes
Baking: 25-30 minutes
Yield: 4 dozen small triangles

4 eggs, slightly beaten
2 cups grated, unpeeled
** zucchini**
1 cup biscuit baking mix
½ cup finely chopped onion
½ cup grated Parmesan
** cheese**
2 tablespoons parsley
½ teaspoon salt
½ teaspoon seasoned salt
½ teaspoon oregano
½ cup vegetable oil
pepper and garlic powder to
** taste**

- Preheat oven to 350°.
- Spray 9x13-inch baking pan with non-stick vegetable spray.
- Mix all ingredients.
- Spread in prepared pan.
- Bake 25-30 minutes.
- Cut into triangles and serve warm.

Mini Potato Skins

"Mini's" are easier to eat than traditional "skins". Quantity of ingredients will vary based on amount you wish to serve.

Preparation: 15 minutes
Baking: 35 minutes
Yield: as many as you would like!

baking potatoes
butter, softened
diced, cooked bacon or taco
** meat**
Cheddar cheese (and/or other
** favorite cheeses)**
green and red bell pepper,
** chopped**
green onion, chopped
sour cream

- Preheat oven to 400°.
- Scrub potatoes and cut crosswise into ¼-inch slices.
- Brush both sides with butter and place on baking sheet.
- Bake 30 minutes or until fork-tender.
- Remove from oven and spread with cheese and meat. Sprinkle with peppers and green onions.
- Return to oven for 2-3 minutes or until cheese is melted.
- Dollop with sour cream or serve it on the side.

Stuffed Potatoes

"Halve" your potato and eat it too!

Preparation: 20 minutes plus chilling
Baking: 45 minutes plus reheating
Yield: 40 appetizers

20 small red potatoes
3 tablespoons butter, room temperature
6 ounces cream cheese, room temperature
¼ cup sour cream
2 ounces Gruyère cheese, shredded
2 tablespoons minced parsley
3 green onions, minced, tops included
1 teaspoon dried basil, crumbled
1 teaspoon garlic powder
¼ cup chopped green onion, tops included

- Preheat oven to 400°.
- Wash potatoes, scrubbing until clean.
- Place potatoes on baking sheet and bake until tender, about 45 minutes.
- Cool slightly.
- Cut in half cross-wise.
- Hollow out potato, leaving ¼-inch shell intact.
- Mash removed potato in mixing bowl.
- Add butter to potato pulp, mixing until butter is melted.
- Using electric mixer, beat cream cheese and sour cream together until fluffy.
- Mix in Gruyère cheese, parsley, minced green onion, basil and garlic powder.
- Stir cheese mixture into potato mixture.
- Spoon stuffing into potato shells.
- Butter large baking dish.
- Arrange potatoes in prepared dish.
- Cover and chill one hour. (These can be prepared to this point up to 2 days before serving.)
- Preheat oven to 325°.
- Bake potatoes until heated through, approximately 20 minutes.
- Sprinkle with green onions and serve warm.

Spinach and Cheese Squares

Try these for Sunday brunch.

*Preparation: 20 minutes plus setting
    time
Baking: 30 minutes
Freezes well
Yield: 40 squares*

¼ **cup butter or margarine**
1 cup flour
3 eggs
1 cup milk
1 teaspoon salt
1 teaspoon baking powder
1 teaspoon dry mustard
**2 (10 ounce) packages frozen
    spinach, thawed, drained
    and squeezed dry**
**8 ounces Monterey Jack
    cheese, shredded**
**8 ounces mozzarella cheese,
    shredded**

• Preheat oven to 350°.
• Melt butter in 9x13-inch baking pan in
  oven.
• In large mixing bowl, combine flour, eggs,
  milk, salt, baking powder and mustard.
  Mix well.
• Add spinach and cheeses; pour in pan.
• Bake 30 minutes.
• When set, cut into squares and serve
  warm.
• Squares may be frozen on baking sheet,
  then placed in freezer container. To serve,
  reheat at 350° for 12 minutes.

Spinach Balls

Popeye's favorite!

Preparation: 25 minutes plus chilling
Baking: 20 minutes
Freezes well before baking
Yield: 40 appetizers

2 (10 ounce) packages frozen chopped spinach, thawed, drained and squeezed dry
¾ cup butter, melted
4½ cups shredded Cheddar cheese
½ teaspoon garlic powder
½ teaspoon thyme
2 cups herb-seasoned stuffing mix
1 cup chopped onion
4 eggs, beaten

- Combine all ingredients.
- Refrigerate 2 hours.
- Preheat oven to 350°.
- Roll mixture into bite-size balls and place on baking sheet.
- Bake 20 minutes.
- Serve warm with Pat's Mustard Sauce.
- To freeze, place unbaked Spinach Balls in freezer on baking sheets. When frozen, place in airtight container in freezer until ready to bake.

Pat's Mustard Sauce

Nice complement to many appetizers.

Preparation: 5 minutes
Yield: 1¾ cups

1 cup mayonnaise
½ cup light cream or half-and-half
2 tablespoons Dijon mustard
2 tablespoons steak sauce
2 tablespoons Worcestershire sauce

- Combine all ingredients and mix well.
- Chill until serving time.

Spinach Phyllo Squares

Be sure to check instructions for thawing phyllo dough—it may take up to 14 hours.

Preparation: 45 minutes to prepare plus thawing time
Baking: 1 hour
Yield: 36 squares

1 pound phyllo dough, thawed as package directs
2 (10 ounce) packages frozen chopped spinach
olive oil
1½ cups chopped onion
½ cup chopped green onion
8 ounces feta cheese, crumbled
5 eggs, beaten
½ tablespoon dillweed
¼ cup parsley
salt and pepper to taste
1 cup butter, melted

- Preheat oven to 350°.
- Cook spinach; squeeze out all moisture.
- Sauté all onions in olive oil in large pan; drain.
- Mix spinach, cheese, eggs, dillweed and parsley. Add drained onions.
- Add salt and pepper to taste.
- In 9x13-inch baking pan, layer half of the phyllo dough, brushing each layer lightly with melted butter. Unused phyllo dough should be wrapped in a damp cloth towel until ready to use.
- Spread filling over phyllo layers and top with remaining phyllo dough, brushing each layer with melted butter.
- Score top for easier cutting when cool.
- Bake 1 hour.

Cheese Triangles

Makes enough for several parties. Be sure to thaw phyllo dough a day ahead.

Preparation: 2 hours plus thawing
Baking: 15 minutes
Freezes well before baking
Yield: 100 triangles

1 pound cream cheese, softened
8 ounces feta cheese, crumbled
¼ cup minced parsley
2 egg yolks
dash of nutmeg
white pepper to taste
3 tablespoons unsalted butter, melted
1 pound phyllo dough, thawed in refrigerator as directed on package
1 cup unsalted butter, melted for brushing on pastry

- Preheat oven to 350°.
- Combine all ingredients except dough and 1 cup melted butter.
- Remove dough from plastic wrapper and place between sheets of heavy plastic wrap to prevent drying out.
- Place one sheet phyllo dough on flat surface and brush with melted butter.
- Fold in half with shorter sides together.
- Cut into strips about 2 inches wide.
- Place 1 teaspoon cheese mixture into corner of phyllo strip.
- Fold opposite side over to form a triangle.
- Continue folding in triangles to end of strip (similar to folding a flag).
- Repeat until all strips and cheese are used.
- Brush triangle tops with butter.
- Place on baking sheet.
- Bake 15 minutes (25 minutes, if frozen) or until golden brown.

Sizzling Cheese Squares

Quick and cheesy.

Preparation: 15-20 minutes
Baking: 5 minutes
Yield: 20-25 squares

1 cup shredded mozzarella cheese
¼ cup real bacon bits
¼ cup mayonnaise
¼ cup chopped black olives
1 tablespoon chives
⅛ cup chopped sweet red pepper
1 loaf party rye bread

- Combine all ingredients except bread.
- Spread on bread.
- Melt under broiler about 5 minutes.

Criqui Quickies

Thanks to Don Criqui, a well-known sports commentator and Notre Dame graduate.

Preparation: 10 minutes
Yield: 48 servings

1 cup shredded Cheddar cheese
3 tablespoons mayonnaise
½ small onion, chopped
½ cup chopped pimiento-stuffed olives
1 tablespoon parsley flakes
1 tablespoon bacon bits (optional)
bread, crust removed

• Combine all ingredients except bread; mix well.
• Cover and refrigerate 2-3 hours.
• Toast bread in oven; cut each slice into 4 pieces.
• Spread cheese mixture over each piece of bread; broil until bubbly.
• Serve immediately.
• Cheese mixture will keep up to 1 week in refrigerator.

Cheese Bread Squares

Great for children.

Preparation: 30 minutes
Baking: 20 minutes
Freezes well before baking
Yield: 65-70 squares

2 (5 ounce) jars sharp pasteurized process cheese spread
1 cup butter, softened
dash of hot pepper sauce
2 loaves sandwich bread

• Preheat oven to 350°.
• Whip together cheese spread, butter, and hot pepper sauce.
• Cut crusts from bread.
• Spread 3 slices of bread with cheese mixture.
• Stack slices and cut into quarters.
• Continue with rest of bread.
• Place on ungreased baking sheet.
• Bake 20 minutes (25 minutes, if frozen).

River Bend Cheese Puffs

*Keep these on hand for
impromptu entertaining.*

*Preparation: 15-20 minutes plus
    freezing time*
Baking: 10-15 minutes
Yield: 40 puffs

½ cup butter, softened
3 ounces Cheddar cheese,
    shredded, room
    temperature
⅔ cup flour
1 pound ricotta cheese
1 teaspoon salt
¼ teaspoon pepper
2 tablespoons dried parsley
1 egg

- Blend butter and Cheddar cheese.
- Add remaining ingredients and combine
  with mixer.
- Drop by teaspoonfuls onto baking sheet.
- Freeze until firm. Put in bags and return to
  freezer until ready to use.
- Preheat oven to 450°. Bake 10-15 min-
  utes.

Toasted Ravioli

This a a St. Louis creation.

Preparation: 1 hour
Yield: 70 appetizers

vegetable oil for deep-frying
2 (9 ounce) packages fresh
    ravioli (about 70 pillows)
½ cup milk
1 cup dry bread crumbs
½ cup grated Parmesan
    cheese
3 cups red Italian meat sauce
    for dipping

- Heat oil in deep fryer or deep pot to 375°.
- Boil ravioli according to package direc-
  tions.
- Drain ravioli and place in single layer on a
  cookie sheet.
- Pour milk into a small dish.
- Place bread crumbs in a separate dish.
- Dip ravioli in milk and then in bread
  crumbs.
- Deep fry the pasta in hot oil until done,
  about 3 or 4 minutes or until golden
  brown. Turn squares as they fry to pro-
  mote even cooking.
- Remove from oil. Drain well.
- Sprinkle with Parmesan cheese.
- Serve with sauce as a dipper.

Cheese Bread

Adds zest to a meal!

Preparation: 10 minutes
Baking: 30 minutes
Yield: 10 appetizer servings

1 (1 pound) loaf Italian, Vienna or French bread
8 ounces Swiss cheese
1 cup butter or margarine
2 tablespoons chopped onion
1 tablespoon dry mustard
1 teaspoon lemon juice
¼ teaspoon salt
1 tablespoon poppy seeds

- Preheat oven to 350°.
- Slice bread in 1-inch slices almost to the bottom, leaving bottom crust intact.
- Line baking sheet with aluminum foil.
- Place bread on foil and pull foil up around bread, leaving top open.
- Slice cheese and place between bread slices.
- Melt margarine and stir in remaining ingredients.
- Pour margarine mixture over bread.
- Bake 30 minutes. Serve warm.

French Bread Monterey

A man pleaser!

Preparation: 20 minutes
Baking: 10 minutes plus browning
Yield: 20 appetizer servings

1 large loaf French bread, unsliced
1 cup mayonnaise
½ cup grated Parmesan cheese
½ cup finely chopped onion
½ teaspoon Worcestershire sauce
paprika

- Preheat oven to 200°.
- Cut bread in half, lengthwise.
- Mix mayonnaise, Parmesan cheese, onion and Worcestershire sauce.
- Spread mixture on both halves of bread.
- Sprinkle with paprika.
- Place in oven for 10 minutes, then turn on broiler and delicately brown.
- Cut at 1½-inch intervals, diagonally.

Note: A little red pepper will add more spice.

Mexican Quiche Appetizer

This could double as a quiche for brunch.

Preparation: 5 minutes
Baking: 30-45 minutes
Yield: 35 squares

4 ounces chopped green chiles
1 pound Cheddar cheese, shredded
1 pound Monterey Jack cheese, shredded
12 eggs, well beaten
6 green onions, chopped
sliced black olives
paprika
1 cup sour cream
salsa

• Preheat oven to 350°.
• Layer chiles and cheese in buttered 9x13-inch baking pan.
• Combine beaten eggs and green onions.
• Pour mixture over chiles and cheese.
• Garnish with black olives and paprika.
• Bake 30-45 minutes.
• Spread sour cream over top. Cut into squares and cool. Serve with salsa.

Gouda Wellington

Makes a great accompaniment to a soup supper.

Preparation: 20 minutes
Baking: 30 minutes
Yield: 4-6 servings

1 (8 ounce) package refrigerated crescent rolls
1 (7 ounce) Gouda cheese
⅓ cup apricot preserves or jam
1 egg white, beaten
sesame seeds for garnish

• Preheat oven to 350°.
• Using fingers, firmly press perforations on dough to seal and form a solid rectangle.
• Remove casing from Gouda cheese. Place in center of dough.
• Cover cheese with preserves or jam.
• Fold dough around cheese, sealing tightly to avoid leaking.
• Brush top with beaten egg white. Garnish with sesame seeds.
• Bake 30 minutes or until brown.
• Allow to set a few minutes. Cut into wedges and serve warm with French bread or crackers.

Camembert in Cream Cheese Pastry

Easy and delicious.

Preparation: 20 minutes plus overnight chilling
Baking: 20 minutes
Yield: 4-8 servings

½ **cup flour**
2 ounces cream cheese, softened
¼ **cup butter, softened**
1 (8 ounce) Camembert cheese round
1 egg yolk

- In a food processor, blend flour, cream cheese, and butter.
- Shape into ball and flatten slightly.
- Wrap well in plastic and refrigerate overnight.
- About 3 hours before serving, roll out pastry to ⅛-inch thickness.
- Cut out 7-inch circle.
- Place on cookie sheet and put cheese in center.
- Bring pastry over top and press until smooth.
- Roll out trimmings and cut another circle for top.
- In small bowl, beat egg yolk with a little water.
- Brush egg yolk on top of pastry.
- Cut decorative pieces from trimmings and arrange on top.
- Brush with egg mixture.
- Refrigerate at least 1 hour.
- Preheat oven to 450°.
- Bake 20 minutes.
- Cool 30 minutes. Cut into wedges to serve.

Variation: Brie cheese may be substituted for Camembert.

Puff Pastry Trio

For true blue cheese lovers.

Preparation: 20 minutes
Baking: 20 minutes
Yield: 8-10 servings

2 tablespoons butter
2 tablespoons flour
½ cup milk
pinch of freshly grated
**   nutmeg**
½ cup grated Gruyère cheese
¼ cup crumbled goat cheese
¼ cup crumbled Gorgonzola
**   cheese**
1 sheet frozen puff pastry,
**   thawed**
1 egg, beaten

- Preheat oven to 475°.
- Melt butter in a small pan.
- Add flour and cook 2 minutes, stirring constantly. Do not brown.
- Slowly add the milk, stirring constantly until thickened and smooth.
- Add nutmeg. Stir to blend. Let cool.
- Combine all the cheeses. Add cheeses to sauce and mix well.
- Roll out the pastry as thinly as possible.
- Cut 2 circles from the dough (one 6 inches, one 7 inches).
- Place the 6-inch circle on a baking sheet.
- Place cheese mixture in center of 6-inch circle. Spread out slightly.
- Moisten edges with water, place 7-inch pastry circle on top, and press down to seal edges.
- Use any scraps of pastry to decorate the top.
- Brush with egg carefully (avoid getting egg on baking sheet).
- Bake at 475° for 10 minutes. Reduce oven temperature to 375° and bake for an additional 10 minutes or until browned.
- Cool on wire rack.

Baked Apricot Brie

Terrific warm or cold.

Preparation: 10 minutes
Baking: 25 minutes
Yield: 6 servings

1 pound round of Brie cheese
1 sheet frozen puff pastry,
**   thawed**
⅓ cup apricot preserves
1 egg, beaten with water

- Preheat oven to 375°.
- On a lightly floured surface, roll dough out enough to assure that it will cover cheese.
- Place Brie in center of puff pastry on baking sheet.
- Spread preserves over cheese.
- Wrap pastry around cheese decoratively, folding ends securely on top.
- Brush with egg mixture.
- Can be refrigerated for several hours at this point.
- Bake 25 minutes.
- Cool for at least 30 minutes before serving.
- Serve warm or cold with crackers or melba toast.

Sweet Hot Brie

Elegant but easy.

Preparation: 10 minutes
Baking: 10 minutes
Yield: 12 servings

1 (1½ pound) round of Brie
**   cheese, not fully ripened**
½ cup chopped pecans
1 cup firmly packed brown
**   sugar**

- Preheat oven to 425°.
- Remove only top rind from cheese.
- Place Brie in 10-inch quiche dish or pie plate.
- Mix pecans and brown sugar together.
- Cover top and sides of Brie with nut and sugar mixture.
- Bake 10 minutes.
- Serve immediately with crackers.

Brie with Sun-Dried Tomatoes

Wonderful, spicy, and lots of great garlic.

Preparation: 1 hour 30 minutes
Yield: 6-8 servings

1 pound Brie cheese, chilled
2 tablespoons minced fresh parsley
2 tablespoons freshly grated Parmesan cheese
4 sun-dried tomatoes, packed in oil, drained and minced (reserve 1 tablespoon of oil)
6 cloves garlic, minced and mashed into a paste
1 teaspoon dried basil, crumbled (or 4 fresh leaves)

- Remove rind from Brie with a sharp knife.
- Place Brie on a serving plate.
- In a small bowl, combine parsley, Parmesan cheese, tomatoes, garlic, and basil.
- Add reserved oil and combine well.
- Spread mixture over Brie and let stand at room temperature 1 hour before serving.
- Serve with French bread rounds or crackers.

Stuffed Brie

Simple to make, gourmet taste.

Preparation: 30 minutes
Yield: 20 servings

**1 (6-8 inch) round of Brie
cheese**
2 tablespoons Pesto
1 tablespoon butter, melted
**¼ cup (1 ounce) almonds or
pinenuts, toasted**

- Freeze Brie for about ½ hour or until firm.
- Cut Brie in half horizontally.
- Spread Pesto over half of cheese.
- Replace remaining half on top.
- Brush Brie with melted butter and cover with toasted nuts.
- Serve at room temperature with French bread rounds or crackers.

Pesto
**2 cups (packed down) fresh
basil or spinach**
2-3 cloves garlic
1 cup olive oil
1 teaspoon salt
**freshly ground pepper to
taste**
**½ cup grated Parmesan
cheese**

- Place all ingredients except cheese in food processor. Process until paste consistency.
- Add cheese, pulse just enough to mix.
- This makes approximately 2 cups of Pesto. Remainder stores well in refrigerator in glass container. Cover with ¼ cup olive oil to keep from turning dark.
- Serve leftovers with your favorite pasta.

Picnic Sandwich

Our photographers loved this!

Preparation: 20 minutes plus thawing time
Baking: 25 minutes
Yield: 16 appetizer servings

1 (1 pound) loaf frozen bread dough
4 ounces each cooked ham, cotto salami, pickle and pimiento loaf or your favorite luncheon meats, sliced thin
8 ounces ricotta cheese
6 ounces provolone cheese or Monterey Jack cheese, coarsely shredded
1 medium onion, chopped
½ cup chopped green bell pepper
½ cup chopped red bell pepper
1 teaspoon oregano

- Let frozen dough thaw to room temperature.
- Preheat oven to 350°.
- Cut meats into ¼-inch wide strips.
- Mix meats, cheeses, onion, chopped peppers and oregano.
- On lightly floured surface, roll dough to 10x14-inch rectangle.
- Place dough on lightly greased baking sheet.
- Spread meat filling in center of dough.
- Bring edges to center and seal.
- Turn over to hide seam.
- Make slits on top of loaf.
- If desired, brush with egg wash and sprinkle with sesame or poppy seeds.
- Bake immediately for 25 minutes or until golden brown.
- Cool on rack to ensure crispy bottom.

Variation: 2-3 ounces sliced olives may be added.

Cucumber Appetizers

So simple yet so good!

Preparation: 10-15 minutes
Yield: about 30 appetizers

1 package dry Italian dressing mix
8 ounces cream cheese, softened
1 loaf party rye bread
2 large cucumbers, sliced

- Blend dressing mix with cream cheese.
- Spread mixture on rye bread slices and top with a cucumber slice.

Shrimp Vinaigrette Wrapped in Snow Peas

Your guests will beg for more.
Very elegant.

Preparation: 1 hour
Marinating: 24-48 hours
Yield: 28-30 wrapped shrimp

1 pound (28-30) raw shrimp
⅓ cup olive oil
3 tablespoons white wine
    vinegar
3 tablespoons Dijon mustard
1½ tablespoons chopped
    shallots or scallions
¾-1 teaspoon finely minced
    ginger
1 clove garlic, finely minced
1 tablespoon fresh dill,
    chopped, or 1½ teaspoons
    dried dillweed
¼ teaspoon salt
⅛ teaspoon pepper
15-20 fresh snow peas

- Bring large pot of water to a boil. Add shrimp. Cover pot and let simmer about 3 minutes. Do not overcook.
- Drain shrimp and run under cold water until chilled. Peel and devein shrimp.
- Combine olive oil, vinegar, mustard, shallots, ginger, garlic, dill, salt and pepper; mix well.
- Place shrimp in a flat glass dish. Pour vinaigrette mixture over shrimp, coating shrimp well.
- Cover and refrigerate 24-48 hours, stirring 2 or 3 times.
- String peapods and blanch in boiling water 30 seconds.
- Drain peapods, immerse in ice water for a few minutes, and drain again.
- Split peapods lengthwise, creating 30-40 halves.
- Wrap a peapod around each marinated shrimp and fasten with a toothpick.
- Arrange in single layer on platter when serving.

Shrimp Relish

Easy—easy!

Preparation: 15 minutes plus marinating
Yield: about 20 appetizers

1½ pounds shrimp, cooked
    and cleaned
1 cup minced onion
1 cup snipped fresh parsley
⅔ cup vegetable oil
⅔ cup vinegar
1 clove garlic, minced
2 teaspoons garlic salt
pepper to taste

- Combine all ingredients and marinate at least overnight.
- Serve with frilled toothpicks.

Marinated Shrimp

Attractive first course for dinner party.

Preparation: 30 minutes plus marinating
Yield: 12-16 servings

2 pounds fresh raw shrimp
2 medium onions, thinly sliced
1½ cups white vinegar
1½ cups vegetable oil
½ cup sugar
1½ teaspoons salt
1½ teaspoons celery seed
¼ cup capers with juice
6 bay leaves

- Peel and devein shrimp.
- Simmer shrimp 3 minutes or until pink in 1 quart of boiling water.
- Drain and rinse in cold water; chill in refrigerator.
- When cold, alternate layers of shrimp and onion in airtight container.
- Mix remaining ingredients and pour over shrimp.
- Seal and refrigerate 6 or more hours, shaking every hour or so.
- Remove from marinade and serve with frilled toothpicks.

Shrimp Rémoulade

Makes a lovely luncheon salad.

Preparation: 30 minutes plus chilling
Yield: 12 servings

¾ cup margarine
¾ cup chili sauce
6 tablespoons horseradish
¾ cup sour cream
3 tablespoons chopped chives
2 tablespoons chopped parsley
1 tablespoon Beau Monde seasoning
1 medium yellow onion, sliced paper thin
3 pounds shrimp, cooked, peeled and deveined
lettuce, for garnish

- Combine all ingredients except lettuce and shrimp; mix well.
- Add shrimp; stir to coat.
- Refrigerate 4 hours or overnight.
- Serve on a bed of lettuce.

Crab Salad Cream Puffs

Make larger puffs and serve at lunch.

Preparation: 2 hours
Baking: 15 minutes
Yield: 40 small puffs

Cream Puffs

½ cup butter or margarine
1 cup boiling water
1 cup flour
¼ teaspoon salt
4 eggs

- Preheat oven to 400 degrees.
- In large saucepan, melt butter in boiling water.
- Add flour and salt all at once. Stir vigorously.
- Cook and stir until mixture forms a ball that does not separate.
- Remove from heat and cool 10 minutes.
- Add eggs, one at a time, beating until smooth after each addition.
- Drop teaspoonfuls of dough 3 inches apart on greased baking sheet.
- Bake 15 minutes. Cool on rack.
- Cut off the top third of each puff. Remove any soft dough from inside.
- Fill each puff with crab salad or your favorite filling and replace puff top. Serve immediately.

Crab Salad Filling

2 (6½ ounce) cans lump crabmeat, drained
1 cup finely chopped celery
2 tablespoons finely chopped onion
1 cup mayonnaise

- Combine all ingredients and mix well.

Variation: Cooked peas, cheese, and sweet pickles make delicious additions.

Tortilla Pinwheels

Great south of the border finger food.

Preparation: 20 minutes plus chilling
Yield: 50 appetizers

8 ounces cream cheese, softened
1 cup sour cream
3 tablespoons medium picante sauce
1 (4 ounce) can chopped green chiles
¼ cup chopped black olives
1 cup (4 ounces) shredded Cheddar cheese
dash of garlic powder
dash of seasoned salt
5 ten-inch flour tortillas
fresh parsley to garnish

- In a medium bowl, mix cream cheese, sour cream, picante sauce, chiles, black olives, cheese, garlic powder and salt.
- Spread ⅕ of cream cheese mixture on each tortilla.
- Roll up and wrap in plastic.
- Chill overnight.
- Slice ½-inch thick and serve on a bed of parsley.

Variation: Add chopped tomato or green onions for "zing".

Vegetable Pizza

Use all red and green toppings for a holiday look.

Preparation: 45 minutes
Baking: 10 minutes
Yield: 20 servings

2 (8 ounce) packages refrigerated crescent rolls
1 pound cream cheese, softened
⅔ cup mayonnaise
1 teaspoon dillweed
¼ teaspoon onion salt
¼ teaspoon garlic powder
¼ teaspoon prepared mustard
favorite fresh vegetables, cut into bite-size pieces
shredded cheese, optional

- Preheat oven to 400°.
- Spread rolls on ungreased baking sheet.
- Seal perforations together to cover baking sheet.
- Bake 10 minutes; cool.
- Mix together cream cheese, mayonnaise, seasonings and mustard. Spread over cooled crust.
- Place assorted vegetables over cheese mixture, randomly or by design, patting vegetables lightly into cheese mixture.
- Top with shredded cheese, if desired. Cut into squares.
- Refrigerate if not used immediately.

Cheese Straws

This a great munchy.

Preparation: 30 minutes
Baking: 15 minutes
Yield: 40 straws

**1½ sheets frozen puff pastry,
    thawed**
1 egg
salt and pepper to taste
**½ cup finely grated
    Emmenthal cheese**

- Preheat oven to 400°.
- Divide puff pastry into 3 equal pieces. On a floured surface, roll out each piece to a 14x5-inch rectangle.
- Beat egg with salt and pepper.
- Brush each rectangle generously with the egg mixture.
- Sprinkle half the cheese over 1 rectangle and cover with second rectangle. Sprinkle with remaining cheese and cover with remaining rectangle.
- Press dough firmly together and cut into thin strips about ¼-inch wide. If dough becomes too sticky or difficult to cut, refrigerate 10-15 minutes.
- Sprinkle a baking sheet with cold water.
- Twist strips of cheese dough and place on baking sheet.
- Refrigerate 15 minutes.
- Bake 15 minutes or until golden.
- Serve with pizza sauce as a dip.

Marinated Mushrooms

Easy—easy—easy!

Preparation: 10 minutes plus marinating
Yield: 2 pounds mushrooms

**approximately 2 pounds fresh
    mushrooms, cleaned**
**1 (8 ounce) bottle Italian
    salad dressing**

- Fill a 3-quart saucepan about half full with water. Bring water to a boil.
- Add cleaned mushrooms; return just to the boil.
- Drain immediately.
- Put mushrooms and salad dressing in tightly sealed plastic container or zippered plastic bag.
- Marinate 24 hours.
- Serve with toothpicks.

Taco Pie

Layers look pretty when unmolded.

Preparation: 30 minutes plus chilling
Yield: 12-15 servings

1 (16 ounce) can refried beans
2 cups sour cream
1 package taco seasoning
2 cups (8 ounces) shredded mozzarella cheese
2 cups (8 ounces) shredded mild Cheddar or colby cheese
3 avocados, peeled and chopped
3 tablespoons lemon juice
mild or hot picante sauce, to taste
4 tomatoes, peeled and chopped
2 bunches green onions, chopped
¼ cup chopped black olives

- Spread beans on bottom of 9-inch or 10-inch springform pan.
- Mix sour cream and taco seasoning; spread over beans.
- Layer cheeses over sour cream mixture.
- Mash avocados with fork; mix with lemon juice and picante sauce. Spread over cheeses.
- Top with tomatoes, then green onions and olives.
- Refrigerate 3-4 hours or overnight.
- Remove sides from pan when ready to serve.
- Serve with tortilla chips.

Mexican Cheesecake

What a combination! Mexican and Cheesecake!!

Preparation: 15 minutes
Baking: 35-40 minutes
Yield: 10 servings

**1 pound cream cheese,
    softened**
**2 cups (8 ounces) shredded
    sharp Cheddar cheese**
2 cups sour cream, divided
**1½ packages taco seasoning
    mix**
3 eggs, room temperature
**1 (4 ounce) can green chiles,
    drained and chopped**
⅔ cup salsa

- Preheat oven to 350°.
- In large bowl, combine cheeses. Beat until fluffy.
- Stir in 1 cup sour cream and taco seasoning.
- Beat in eggs, one at a time, mixing well after each addition.
- Fold in chiles.
- Pour into 9-inch springform pan.
- Bake 35-40 minutes or until center is firm.
- Remove from oven. Cool 10 minutes.
- Spoon remaining 1 cup sour cream over cheesecake.
- Bake 5 minutes longer. Cool completely.
- Cover and refrigerate several hours.
- Before serving, remove sides of springform pan and top with salsa.
- Serve with plain taco chips.

Home Fried Tortillas

*A "must" with any good
Mexican dip.*

Preparation: 40 minutes
Yield: 160 chips

**4 (6 ounce) packages 5-inch
    corn tortillas**
**3 cups butter-flavored solid
    shortening for frying**
salt to taste

- Cut each tortilla into 4 triangles (a total of 160 triangles).
- Melt shortening in deep, heavy skillet. Heat until bubbling.
- Add 10-12 triangles at a time to shortening. Turn once triangles float to top, about 30 seconds.
- Watch carefully as tortillas burn easily.
- Remove chips when shortening stops bubbling.
- Place on paper towel-lined cookie sheets and salt while still warm.
- Store in large plastic bag for up to 1 week.

Taco Dip

Once you start eating, you just can't stop.

Preparation: 30 minutes
Yield: 10-15 servings

2-3 medium tomatoes
salt and pepper to taste
1 pound cream cheese, softened
2 cups sour cream
1 (1¼ ounce) package hot and spicy taco seasoning
2 (8 ounce) bottles medium taco sauce
3 cups shredded lettuce
8 ounces Cheddar cheese, shredded
1 bunch (5-7) green onions, chopped
1 (3 ounce) can sliced black olives

- Chop tomatoes in ¼- to ½-inch chunks. Add salt and pepper to taste.
- Put in colander to drain while preparing remaining ingredients.
- Mix cream cheese, sour cream, and taco seasoning until smooth.
- Spread in large serving dish.
- Cover with 1½-2 bottles taco sauce.
- Layer remaining ingredients in order: lettuce, cheese, tomatoes, green onions, and black olives.
- Serve with corn tortilla chips.
- May be prepared 8-12 hours ahead and refrigerated.

Easy Guacamole

Keeps color well for several hours.

Preparation: 20 minutes
Yield: 3 cups

2 avocados, peeled and chopped
¾-1 cup mayonnaise
1 small onion, minced
2 tablespoons salsa
1 tablespoon lime or lemon juice
dash of hot pepper sauce
1-2 tomatoes, peeled and chopped

- Combine all ingredients, except tomatoes, in food processor; blend until smooth.
- Add tomatoes and blend just until tomatoes are in small chunks.
- Serve with tortilla chips.

Avocado Salsa

Not your ordinary salsa.

Preparation: 30 minutes plus standing time
Yield: 3½-4 cups

1 tablespoon vegetable oil
3 tablespoons wine vinegar
1½ teaspoons seasoned salt
dash of chili powder
dash of hot pepper sauce
3 ripe tomatoes, diced
6-8 green onions, sliced very
  thin
¼ cup chopped cilantro
2-3 ripe avocados, peeled
  and diced just before
  serving

- Combine vegetable oil, vinegar, seasoned salt, chili powder and hot pepper sauce. Mix well.
- Gently add tomatoes, green onions, and cilantro. Let stand at room temperature for 1½ to 2 hours.
- Before serving, peel and dice avocados and add to tomato mixture.
- Serve with warm tortilla chips.

Crab and Avocado Mexicali

This makes a great luncheon salad served on a bed of tortilla chips.

Preparation: 15 minutes
Yield: 2½ cups

3 avocados, peeled, pitted
  and cubed
⅓ cup chopped green onions
⅓ cup sour cream
3-4 tablespoons fresh lemon
  or lime juice
salt, pepper and hot pepper
  sauce to taste
½ pound cooked crabmeat,
  chopped

- Combine avocado, green onions, sour cream, lemon or lime juice and seasonings. Mix gently.
- Fold in crabmeat.
- Serve with tortilla chips.

Shrimply Divine Dip

The name says it all!

Preparation: 10 minutes plus chilling
Yield: 3 cups

**6 ounces cream cheese,
    softened**
1 cup sour cream
2 teaspoons lemon juice
**1 (⅝ ounce) package dry
    Italian salad dressing mix**
**1 medium green pepper,
    finely chopped**
**2 (4½ ounce) cans shrimp,
    rinsed, drained and finely
    chopped**

• Combine cream cheese, sour cream,
  lemon juice and dry dressing mix; blend
  thoroughly.
• Stir in green pepper and shrimp.
• Chill at least 1 hour before serving.
• Serve with crackers.

Shrimp Butter

Always a hit!

Preparation: 5 minutes
Yield: 2 cups

**8 ounces cream cheese,
    softened**
**2 (4½ ounce) cans small
    shrimp, rinsed, drained
    and chopped**
**2 tablespoons butter,
    softened**
¼ cup chopped onion
1 tablespoon lemon juice
**2 green onions, chopped, for
    garnish**

• Combine all ingredients, except green
  onions, and beat well.
• Place in serving bowl; sprinkle with green
  onions to garnish.
• Serve with crackers.

Chili Shrimp Dip

Chili sauce adds the zip!

*Preparation: 10 minutes plus chilling
Yield: 2 cups*

**8 ounces cream cheese,
  softened**
6 tablespoons mayonnaise
**1 tablespoon dried minced
  onion**
**1-1½ teaspoons dried minced
  garlic**
1 tablespoon parsley flakes
2 tablespoons chili sauce
**5 ounces frozen cooked
  shrimp, thawed and
  drained**

- Combine cream cheese, mayonnaise, onion, garlic and parsley; blend well.
- Mix in chili sauce.
- Coarsely chop shrimp; stir into cream cheese mixture.
- Chill 2 hours or overnight.
- Serve with crackers.

Polynesian Crab Dip

Makes you want to take a trip to the islands.

*Preparation: 20 minutes plus overnight
  chilling
Yield: 3½-4 cups*

1 cup sour cream
1 cup mayonnaise
1 (6 ounce) can crab, drained
1 cup coconut (optional)
½ cup chopped onion
**1 (4 ounce) can mushrooms,
  drained and chopped**
¼ teaspoon curry powder
**2 tablespoons snipped fresh
  parsley**
salt and pepper to taste
**2 ounces toasted, slivered
  almonds, for garnish**
**fresh pineapple half, with
  leaves intact**

- Thoroughly mix all ingredients, except almonds and pineapple. Chill overnight.
- Scoop out pineapple half leaving ½-inch shell all around. Fill with crab mixture. Garnish with almonds.
- Serve with crackers.

Bacon Tomato Dip

Very pretty served in a tomato shell.

Preparation: 20 minutes plus chilling
Yield: 2 cups

6 slices bacon
8 ounces cream cheese,
    softened
2 teaspoons prepared
    mustard
½ teaspoon celery salt
1 medium tomato, peeled,
    seeded and finely chopped
    (½-¾ cup)
¼ cup finely chopped green
    pepper
milk to thin

- Cook bacon in skillet until crisp. Remove and drain on paper towels. Crumble.
- In a mixing bowl, combine softened cream cheese, mustard, and celery salt.
- Stir in crumbled bacon, tomato, and green pepper.
- Thin with milk, if necessary.
- Transfer to serving bowl. Cover and chill until cold.
- Serve with fresh vegetable dippers.

Bacon Almond Dip

Can be made 2 days ahead.

Preparation: 30 minutes
Yield: 2 cups

1 pound bacon, chopped
½ cup (2 ounces) slivered
    almonds
6 ounces cream cheese,
    softened
1 cup sour cream
1 tablespoon chives
2 tablespoons chili sauce
¼ teaspoon hot pepper sauce
freshly ground pepper to
    taste
¼ cup chopped green onions
milk to thin

- Preheat oven to 350°.
- In a large skillet, fry bacon until crisp, stirring occasionally. Drain on paper towels.
- Toast almonds in oven 10-15 minutes, stirring occasionally.
- In mixing bowl, combine cream cheese, sour cream, chives, chili sauce, hot pepper sauce and pepper. Mix well.
- Add green onions, bacon, and almonds. Mix until blended but still chunky.
- Refrigerate until ready to serve.
- Can be thinned with a little milk if dip is too thick after refrigeration.
- Serve with small bread rounds or crackers.

Raw Asparagus with Cream Cheese Dip

A dip made especially for tender, spring asparagus.

Preparation: 20-30 minutes
Yield: 10 servings

8 ounces cream cheese, softened
½ cup sour cream
3 green onions, minced
2 tablespoons capers
2 tablespoons snipped parsley
1 tablespoon Dijon mustard
pinch tarragon
pinch basil
pinch marjoram
salt and pepper to taste
2 pounds fresh, thin asparagus, washed well and trimmed

- Blend all ingredients, except asparagus, until smooth.
- Cover and chill.
- Serve with asparagus for dipping.

Caviar Pie

An easy make-ahead appetizer

Preparation: 10 minutes plus chilling
Yield: 12 servings

3 hard-boiled eggs, finely chopped
1 small onion, finely chopped
5 tablespoons butter, melted
1 (2 ounce) jar caviar
1 cup sour cream

- Combine eggs and onion with melted butter.
- Line a small soup plate or shallow dish with plastic wrap.
- Press mixture evenly into prepared plate.
- Cover and refrigerate several hours or until firm.
- Can be made to this point up to 2 days ahead.
- When ready to serve, turn mixture out of mold onto serving plate.
- Cover with caviar and a thin layer of sour cream.
- Let stand at room temperature ½ hour before serving.
- Serve with melba toast and lemon wedges.

Holtz Spinach Dip

*Courtesy of Lou Holtz, head
football coach, University of
Notre Dame.*

*Preparation: 15 minutes plus chilling
Yield: 4 cups*

**1 (10 ounce) package frozen
chopped spinach, thawed,
drained and squeezed dry**
**¼-⅓ package dry vegetable
soup mix**
1¾ cups plain non-fat yogurt
¼ cup low-fat mayonnaise
**1 (8 ounce) can water
chestnuts, drained and
chopped**
2 green onions, minced
1 clove garlic, minced
**1 (4-6 ounce) can shrimp,
rinsed and drained**
**1 round loaf sheepherders or
sourdough bread**

- Blend all ingredients except bread. Chill before serving.
- Slice top off loaf and hollow out center.
- Fill bread with chilled dip and serve with Pita Chips and fresh vegetables.

Pita Chips

Wonderful dippers.

*Preparation: 5 minutes
Baking: 5-10 minutes
Yield: as many as you like!*

**whole wheat pita bread, split
in half**
safflower or olive oil
part-skim Parmesan cheese
poppy or sesame seeds

- Preheat oven to 350°.
- Brush pita bread lightly with oil.
- Sprinkle lightly with Parmesan, then with poppy or sesame seeds.
- Cut into 8 wedges.
- Arrange on baking sheet and bake until crisp, 5-10 minutes.

Zesty Cheese Spread

Great on baked potatoes!

Preparation: 10 minutes
Freezes well
Yield: 8-10 servings

**8 ounces cream cheese,
softened**
**¼ cup salad dressing or
mayonnaise**
1 small onion, chopped
2 tablespoons milk
**¼ teaspoon freshly ground
pepper**
**4 drops hot pepper sauce (or
to taste)**
1 teaspoon garlic powder
1 cup shredded colby cheese

• Combine all ingredients and mix well. (May be blended in food processor).
• Thin with 1-2 additional tablespoons of milk, if necessary.
• Serve with crackers or vegetables.
• This may be frozen. To serve, thaw to room temperature and thin with milk to desired consistency.

Cheddar Chutney Pie

A chutney lover's delight.

Preparation: 10 minutes
Yield: 6-8 servings

**8 ounces cream cheese,
softened**
**1 cup (4 ounces) shredded
sharp Cheddar cheese,
room temperature**
¼ cup sherry
**½ teaspoon curry powder, or
to taste**
**½ cup peach or mixed fruit
chutney**
**4 green onions, finely
chopped**

• Combine cheeses well using a mixer or food processor.
• Add sherry and curry powder.
• Place mixture in an 8-inch or 9-inch round quiche dish or pie plate.
• Mixture may be frozen at this point.
• At serving time, spread chutney over cheese mixture.
• Garnish edges with green onions.
• Serve with crackers or pumpernickel bread.

Chicken Pâté Mousse

A delicious but easy version of traditional pâté.

8 slices bacon, diced
1 pound chicken livers
½ cup brandy
¾ cup heavy cream
1 medium onion, chopped
¼ cup mayonnaise
1 teaspoon dried thyme
large pinch ground nutmeg
salt and pepper, to taste
½ cup chopped walnuts
3 tablespoons snipped fresh
　parsley

Preparation: 30 minutes plus overnight chilling
Yield: 3 cups pâté

- Cook bacon until crisp and drain on paper towels.
- Sauté chicken livers in bacon fat over medium heat until browned but still pink inside, 4-5 minutes. Remove from pan and set aside.
- Pour brandy into pan and scrape up loose bacon bits.
- Add cream and bring to a boil. Simmer until 1 cup of liquid remains.
- Put livers, cream and onion into food processor and blend until smooth.
- Add mayonnaise, thyme, nutmeg, salt and pepper; process well.
- Add bacon, walnuts and parsley; process just until blended.
- Put pâté in serving dish, cover and refrigerate overnight.
- Garnish with additional bacon, walnuts and parsley if desired.
- Serve with crackers or crusty bread.

Smoked Salmon Pâté

A food processor makes preparation easy.

⅔ pound smoked salmon
　meat, boned
1 cup butter, softened
1½ tablespoons lemon juice
¼ cup heavy cream
⅛ teaspoon cayenne pepper

Preparation: 30 minutes plus chilling
Yield: 8-10 servings

- In food processor, blend salmon in batches with butter, lemon juice and cream until the mixture is smooth; transfer to bowl as each batch is blended.
- Stir in cayenne pepper.
- Line a narrow mold with plastic wrap.
- Spread salmon mixture in mold.
- Chill pâté, covered, for 8 hours.
- Unmold and serve with toast triangles or your favorite crackers.

Chicken Liver Pâté with Aspic

For traditional pâté lovers!

Preparation: 40 minutes plus overnight chilling
May be frozen
Yield: 3 cups pâté

Pâté

1 pound chicken livers
⅔ cup thinly sliced onion
1 clove garlic, peeled and crushed
2 bay leaves, crushed
¼ teaspoon thyme
1 cup water
2 teaspoons salt, divided
1½ cups butter, softened
freshly ground pepper to taste
2 teaspoons cognac or Scotch
scallions and tomato skin, for garnish

- Combine livers, onion, garlic, bay leaves, thyme, water and 1 teaspoon salt in saucepan.
- Heat until boiling; cover and simmer gently 7-8 minutes. Remove from heat and let stand 5 minutes.
- Remove solids with slotted spoon and put in food processor fitted with a metal blade. Reserve and strain 1 cup liquid to make aspic, if desired.
- Process liver mixture, adding butter in small pieces, until all butter has been added.
- Add remaining 1 teaspoon salt, pepper and cognac.
- Process 2 minutes more until mixture is very creamy and completely smooth. If mixture looks broken down, with visible fat, let it cool in refrigerator for about 1 hour to harden butter, then process again until creamy and smooth.
- Pour into decorative 3-cup serving dish.
- Refrigerate 12 hours or overnight.
- If desired, prepare and add aspic. Garnish with jagged-edged tomato skin pieces and blanched scallions, forming a flower and stem.
- Serve with melba toasts or crackers.

Aspic

1 envelope unflavored gelatin
1 cup strained cooking liquid

- Combine gelatin and 1 cup reserved strained liquid in saucepan.
- Stir gently over low heat until mixture almost boils and gelatin is completely dissolved.
- Put saucepan on ice and stir until liquid becomes very syrupy. Aspic should be shiny and about to set. If aspic becomes too thick, it may be reheated and cooled again over ice.
- Spread 3-4 tablespoons aspic on top of pâté. Aspic should be about ¼-inch thick. Decorate as described.

Note: Pâté may be frozen before the aspic and vegetable decoration are added. Cover tightly with plastic wrap, then aluminum foil. Defrost in refrigerator 24-48 hours, then decorate.

Summer Fruit Dip

Fruit dip for adults.

3 egg yolks
¼ cup plus 2 tablespoons
   sugar
¼ teaspoon salt
1 tablespoon orange-flavored
   liqueur
2 cups whipping cream

Preparation: 15-20 minutes plus chilling
Yield: 4 cups

- In a small saucepan, combine egg yolks, sugar, and salt. Mix well.
- Cook over medium heat, stirring constantly, 2 or 3 minutes until sugar dissolves.
- Remove from heat. Stir in liqueur.
- Set aside to cool.
- In a medium bowl, beat whipping cream until stiff peaks form.
- Fold into cooled liqueur mixture.
- Cover and chill 1-2 hours.
- Serve with assorted fresh fruits.

Macaroon Fruit Dip

This a wonderful summertime appetizer.

2 cups sour cream
3 tablespoons firmly packed
   light brown sugar
10 macaroon cookies, broken
   into small pieces
fresh pineapple half for
   serving

Preparation: 10 minutes plus chilling
Yield: 2½-3 cups

- In a medium bowl, combine sour cream, brown sugar, and cookie pieces. Mix well.
- Refrigerate at least 1½ hours.
- Scoop out center of pineapple, leaving shell intact. Fill center with dip.
- Serve with assorted fresh fruits: strawberries, bananas, apples, melon, and pineapple are especially good.

Ambrosia Dip

Great for brunch or tea.

Preparation: 15-20 minutes
Yield: 2 cups

**1 (11 ounce) can mandarin
oranges, chilled and
drained**
**1 (8 ounce) container soft-
style cream cheese with
pineapple**
¼ cup toasted coconut
**¼ cup toasted chopped
almonds**
whole almonds for garnish

- Reserve several orange sections for
  garnish; chop remaining oranges.
- In medium bowl, stir together chopped
  oranges, cream cheese, coconut and
  chopped almonds.
- Spoon into serving dish. Surround with
  whole almonds and top with reserved
  orange sections.
- Serve with banana or nut bread slices.

Cinnamon Fruit Dip

*Wonderfully simple and simply
wonderful.*

Preparation: 5 minutes
Yield: about 3 cups

**8 ounces cream cheese,
softened**
**1 (13 ounce) jar
marshmallow creme**
1 teaspoon cinnamon
½ teaspoon nutmeg

- Mash cream cheese with a fork.
- Add marshmallow creme and spices. Mix
  well.
- Serve with assorted fresh fruit.

Pineapple Cheese Spread

*Attractive and festive when
served in a pineapple boat.*

*Preparation: 15 minutes
Yield: 3½ cups*

**1 pound cream cheese,
  softened**
**1 (8½ ounce) can crushed
  pineapple, well drained**
1 cup chopped pecans
¼ cup chopped green pepper
2 tablespoons chopped onion
1 teaspoon seasoned salt
**fresh pineapple half (with
  leaves)**

- Beat cream cheese at medium speed until fluffy.
- Stir in crushed pineapple, pecans, green peppers, onion and seasoned salt.
- Hollow out pineapple half leaving a ½-inch rim. Put spread in pineapple boat. Serve with crackers or bread rounds.

*Variation: May be served as cheese balls. To do so, divide mixture in half
and form into 2 balls. Roll in an additional 1 cup of chopped pecans.*

Cheese and Apple Spread

Colorful fall appetizer.

*Preparation: 15 minutes plus chilling
Yield: 2-2½ cups*

**8 ounces cream cheese,
  softened**
**½ cup salad dressing or
  mayonnaise**
**½ cup shredded sharp
  Cheddar cheese**
**½ cup finely chopped Red
  and Golden Delicious
  apples**

- Combine cream cheese and salad dressing. Mix until well blended.
- Add cheese and apples. Mix well.
- Chill 1 hour.
- Serve with apple wedges and crackers.

Cranberry Chutney Cheese Ball

Can be made up to 4 days ahead.

Preparation: 15 minutes plus chilling
Yield: 2 cups

**8 ounces cream cheese,
  softened**
2 tablespoons sour cream
2 teaspoons curry powder
½ cup chopped green onion
½ cup raisins
**½ cup chopped dry roasted
  peanuts**
**1 cup Cranberry Chutney or
  1 (9 ounce) jar chutney**

- Combine cream cheese, sour cream, and curry powder. Mix well.
- Stir in green onions, raisins, and peanuts.
- Form into ball. Refrigerate.
- When ready to serve, pour chutney over top of cheese ball.
- Serve with crackers.

Cranberry Chutney

1¾ cups sugar
1¾ cups water
**4 cups (1 pound) fresh or
  frozen cranberries**
1 cup golden raisins
½ cup red wine vinegar
2 tablespoons molasses
1½ tablespoons curry powder
**1 tablespoon Worcestershire
  sauce**
2 teaspoons ground ginger
1 teaspoon salt
½ teaspoon nutmeg
½ teaspoon hot pepper sauce

- In a medium saucepan, combine sugar and water. Bring to a boil over medium high heat.
- Reduce heat and simmer for 5 minutes.
- Add cranberries. Cook just until skins pop, about 5 minutes.
- Stir in remaining ingredients.
- Simmer uncovered until thickened, about 15 minutes, stirring occasionally.
- Ladle into four 8-ounce jars and seal.
- Once open, store in refrigerator for up to 6 weeks.

Holiday Cheese Ring

A surprising combination.

Preparation: 15 minutes plus chilling
Yield: 15 servings

1 pound sharp Cheddar
   cheese, shredded
¾ cup mayonnaise
1 medium onion, finely
   chopped
1 clove garlic, pressed
½ teaspoon hot pepper sauce
1 cup chopped pecans
1 cup strawberry preserves

- Combine all ingredients except preserves. Mix well.
- Press mixture into 5-cup ring mold. Chill about 4 hours or until firm.
- Unmold onto serving plate. Fill center with preserves.
- Serve with buttery crackers or small pumpernickel bread slices.

Mousse Raifort

Zesty horseradish mold.

Preparation: 15 minutes plus chilling
Yield: 3 cups

1¼ cups slivered almonds,
   divided
2 tablespoons parsley
1 pound cream cheese,
   softened
⅓-½ cup prepared
   horseradish
fresh parsley
lemon zest or grated lemon
   peel

- Combine ¼ cup almonds and 2 tablespoons parsley in food processor. Pulse briefly.
- Add cream cheese and horseradish. Process until well blended.
- Line a loaf pan with plastic wrap. Pat horseradish mixture into prepared pan. Chill at least 1 hour.
- Thirty minutes before serving, invert mold onto serving plate and remove plastic wrap.
- Press remaining slivered almonds around sides. Sprinkle parsley and lemon zest or grated lemon peel down center of mold.
- Serve with thin wheat crackers.

Cream Cheese Chutney Ball

Will make a chutney lover out of you.

Preparation: 30 minutes including chilling
Yield: 2 cups

1 pound cream cheese, softened
1 tablespoon grated onion
6 tablespoons coarsely chopped chutney
¾ cup chopped almonds, toasted

- Combine cream cheese, onion and chutney. Mix well.
- Refrigerate until easy to handle.
- Shape into a ball and roll in almonds.
- Serve with crackers.

Long Beach Island Cheese Ball

Thanks to Digger Phelps, former head basketball coach, University of Notre Dame.

Preparation: 10 minutes
Yield: 1 6-inch cheese ball

8 ounces shredded sharp Cheddar cheese
3 ounces cream cheese
1 tablespoon Worcestershire sauce
2 tablespoons minced onion
1 small jar pimientos, drained
chopped parsley

- Combine all ingredients except parsley in workbowl of food processor and process until mixed.
- Form mixture into a ball.
- Roll in chopped parsley.
- Serve with your favorite crackers.

Blue Cheese Black Olive Cheese Log

Great on any buffet table.

Preparation: 15 minutes plus chilling time
Yield: 1 one-pound cheese log

8 ounces cream cheese, softened
8 ounces blue cheese, crumbled
¼ cup butter, softened
⅔ cup pitted black olives, chopped
1 tablespoon minced chives
slivered almonds

- Combine cheeses, butter, olives, and chives. Mix well.
- Form into a log. Roll in slivered almonds.
- Chill before serving.
- Serve with crackers.

Deviled Ham Cheese Ball

Great energy food for a leaf-raking party!

Preparation: 15 minutes plus chilling
Yield: 3½-4 cups

2 (4¼ ounce) cans deviled ham spread
8 ounces cream cheese, softened
1 package dry ranch-style dressing mix
1 tablespoon horseradish
1 tablespoon minced onion
1 teaspoon dry mustard
2 cups shredded Cheddar cheese

- In a medium mixing bowl, combine all ingredients.
- Refrigerate until firm enough to handle.
- Form into a ball. Refrigerate until ready to serve.
- Serve with crackers or fresh vegetables.

Variation: For an autumn party, turn this cheese ball into a pumpkin! Draw vertical lines on cheese ball, resembling the lines on a pumpkin and add a green pepper stem for the pumpkin's stem.

Shrimp Mold

Dill pickle makes this better than the rest.

6 ounces cream cheese, softened
1 (10¾ ounce) can tomato soup
1 envelope unflavored gelatin
½ cup finely chopped celery
½ cup finely chopped dill pickle
½ cup finely chopped green pepper
½ cup finely chopped green onion
1 cup mayonnaise
2 tablespoons Worcestershire sauce
1 pound cooked medium shrimp, diced in large pieces

Preparation: 30 minutes plus chilling
Yield: 6 cups

- Heat cream cheese and soup in double boiler until melted; cool slightly.
- Stir in gelatin.
- Beat until fluffy, about 1 minute.
- Add celery, pickle, green pepper and onion; mix well.
- Stir in mayonnaise, Worcestershire sauce and shrimp.
- Pour into 6-cup mold and chill for at least 8 hours.
- Unmold and serve with crackers.

Salmon Ball

The nuts make this different and very tasty.

1 (6½ ounce) can salmon, drained
8 ounces cream cheese, softened
2 tablespoons grated onion
1 tablespoon lemon juice
½ cup chopped pecans
1 tablespoon horseradish
¼ cup fresh chopped parsley
lemon slices for garnish

Preparation: 15 minutes
Yield: 1 6-inch ball

- Combine all ingredients, except parsley and lemon; shape into a ball.
- Roll ball in parsley.
- Refrigerate until serving time.
- Surround ball with lemon slices and serve with crackers.

Crabmeat Mold

This is also delicious made with shrimp.

Preparation: 15 minutes plus chilling
Yield: 12-15 servings

2 (6½ ounce) cans crabmeat
1½ pounds cream cheese,
softened
6 tablespoons mayonnaise
¼ teaspoon salt
½ teaspoon curry powder
1 tablespoon lemon juice
1 teaspoon Worcestershire
sauce
2 tablespoons minced fresh
onion
fresh parsley and paprika for
garnish

- Drain crabmeat well; remove and discard tendons. Finely chop crabmeat and set aside.
- Combine cream cheese, mayonnaise, salt, curry powder, lemon juice, Worcestershire sauce and onion; mix well.
- Fold in crabmeat.
- Brush 1½-quart mold lightly with oil.
- Press crabmeat mixture into prepared mold; chill one hour.
- Unmold on serving tray. Garnish with crisp parsley and a sprinkle of paprika.
- Serve with crackers.

Here's to
SOUTH BEND

Shown above (left to right): Cinnamon Fruit Dip (pg. 73),
Shrimp Vinaigrette Wrapped in Peapods (pg. 54),
Apricot Triangles (pg. 198), King-Size Steak Bites (pg. 17),
Parmesan Chicken Wings (pg. 15), Dutch Apple Pie (pg. 159),
Pumpkin Lemon Cream Pie (pg. 160),
Raspberry Cream Cheese Pie (pg. 152), Walnut Pie (pg. 161),
White Chocolate Macadamia Nut Cookies (pg. 196),
Taco Dip (pg. 61).

South Bend, located on the southernmost bend of the Saint Joseph River, has something for everyone: history, culture, industry and education.

Through the years, abundant natural resources and a centralized location encouraged industrial and community development. Despite temptations to become a high pressure city, South Bend remains a hometown with traditional family values.

Sparks of enthusiasm fly each autumn when the Notre Dame victory march proclaims the opening of yet another Irish football season.

Since 1887 when the first Notre Dame team faced the University of Michigan, students, families, alumni and friends have surrounded the stadium with blue and gold, anticipating victory. Tailgating parties complete with finger food and mouth-watering pies get and keep loyal fans energized.

But there is more to get excited about at Notre Dame than football. Since its founding in 1842 by Father Sorin, a French priest, academic excellence has been the cornerstone of the University. The undergraduate programs, as well as the graduate programs and law school, are recognized internationally, and attract students from all over the world. Both the University and South Bend are enriched when they come together, as they often do, to volunteer for worthwhile community projects.

As host to the 1987 International Summer Special Olympics the South Bend community and the Notre Dame campus united to witness a spectacular display of athletic courage and discipline. With the help of the Junior League of South Bend and the community, over 50,000 volunteers, athletes and their families experienced the grandeur of the University as well as some hometown hospitality.

Hoosier Hospitality goes back a long way. During the late nineteenth century, parties and balls were the way to keep in touch with family and friends.

Clement C. Studebaker and James D. Oliver were two of the industrial giants who would sponsor such events at

South Bend's East Race has been restored to serve as a world class whitewater raceway.

Sprinkled throughout the city are many parks perfect for picnicking.

Shown above (left to right): Peanut Butter Pie (pg. 162),
Picnic Sandwich (pg. 53).

*Graduation is celebrated with
delicious food, stories of the past and
dreams for the future.*

Shown front to back: Shrimp Mold (pg. 79),
Asparagus Roll-Ups (pg. 31), Peanut Butter Cups (pg. 213),
Mini Potato Skins (pg. 38), Chicken Fingers with Plum Sauce (pg. 14),
Great-Grandma's Dark Chocolate Cake (pg. 104).

their homes. Studebaker's home, Tippecanoe Place, now houses one of South Bend's finest restaurants. Copshaholm, built by Oliver, is now a living house museum and the showpiece of the Northern Indiana Historical Society.

The Studebakers and the Olivers embodied three distinctive Midwestern values: hard work, honesty and persistence.

Studebaker began as a wagon builder and transformed his company into a nationally recognized automobile business. Oliver, founder of one of several local farm equipment manufacturers, developed and patented the chilled plow. When fire destroyed his facility, the South Bend Iron Works, Oliver did not give up. He rebuilt, and the Oliver Chilled Plow Works became the largest plow factory in the world.

Many turn-of-the-century factories were situated on the East Race of the St. Joseph River, operating on hydro-electric power. Today this man-made canal has been restored to serve as a world class whitewater raceway, *one of only three in the world.*

Sprinkled throughout the city are other parks perfect for picnicking with large shady trees and playgrounds. St. Patrick's County Park is home to the award-winning Firefly Festival, a popular performing arts series held throughout the summer. Families come, spread their blankets, and enjoy a wonderful evening under the stars. Potawatomi Park Zoo features Kid's Kingdom, a child-designed and community-built playground. Junior League provided funding and volunteers to assure the success of both of these family-oriented projects.

Children are a vital part of any community and ours is no exception.

As home to a variety of public and private schools, several colleges and universities, we value learning. Not only is education necessary to pass on our heritage, it is the only way to keep our community moving in a positive direction.

*The Beiger Mansion is a lovely setting
for a bridal shower. Friends and
family enjoy rich chocolate treats
and delicate pastries as they
make plans for the Big Day.*

Shown left to right: Maple Cinnamon Pecans (pg. 212),
Chocolate Truffle Torte (pg. 112), Easy Cut Sugar Cookies (pg. 192),
Turtle Cheesecake (pg. 136).

Who wouldn't wake up on the right side of bed when awakened with Cheese Strudel and Chocolate-Dipped Strawberries?

Shown clockwise: Chocolate-Dipped Strawberries (pg. 214),
Cheese Strudel (pg. 132), French Waffle Cookies (pg. 200).

That's why graduation is a time for celebration. As family and friends offer words of praise and wishes for good luck, the graduate realizes a sense of accomplishment. The party continues with lots of good food, stories of the past and dreams for the future, the doors that are opened and the ones that have closed.

Marriage is another cause for celebration. As the formal arrangements are made, the two families prepare to unite with dinner parties and showers.

At the bridal shower, friends and family enjoy rich chocolate treats and delicate pastries as they make plans for the Big Day. The Beiger Mansion, former home of Martin and Susie Beiger, is a lovely setting for one of these parties.

The Beigers were family and community people. As the co-founder of the Mishawaka Woolen Manufacturing Company which later became part of Uniroyal, Inc., Beiger was a prominent businessman. Although the

Beigers' taste for adventure took them around the world, there was no other place they would call home. When they were able to build the home of their dreams, they filled it with treasures from their travels. The Beiger Mansion is now a bed and breakfast inn. Who wouldn't wake up on the right side of bed when awakened with Cheese Strudel and Chocolate-Dipped Strawberries?

Other home-baked delights await those who travel a short distance east to visit our local Amish and Mennonite communities. Horses and buggies, quilt and antique shops, and restaurants serving hearty wholesome food take one back in time. At harvest time, it is not unusual to see all the members of a family in the fields gathering nature's bounty by hand.

D ue to the tempering effects of Lake Michigan, the fertile land north of South Bend is ideal for growing grapes.

At Tabor Hill and other local wineries, the products of a good harvest call us to partake of their fullness. Just a bite of Baked Apricot Brie with a sip of wine rewards us

The fertile land north of South Bend
is ideal for growing grapes.
The products of a good harvest
remind us that nature has been good
to us once again.

Baked Apricot Brie (pg. 50)

The Firefly Festival is a popular performing arts series held throughout the summer.

Fall is harvest time for the local Amish community.

*for a summer of hard work and reminds us that nature
has been good to us once again.*

T

he South Bend area is also blessed with a wealth of cultural resources.

*Symphonies, operas, plays and dance recitals are just
some of the ways we feed our love of the arts. Fifteen
miles east of South Bend lies Elkhart, Indiana, known as
the "Band Instrument Capital of the World." Over the
years as many as fifty musical instrument manufacturers,
such as Conn, Selmer, and W.T. Armstrong, have located
there. The sousaphone was developed and first manufac-
tured in Elkhart according to John Philip Sousa's specifi-
cations.*

*Elkhart is also home to Miles Laboratories, Inc., a
national pharmaceutical manufacturer. Albert R.
Beardsley is remembered as the first true manager at
Miles. In addition to his affiliation with Miles, Beardsley
was active in civic affairs and held several public offices.
Ruthmere, his home, was undoubtedly the scene of many*

elegant parties. Whether his guests enjoyed Chocolate Walnut Bliss or Lemon Soufflé is hard to say, but friends were always welcome in his home.

A wonderful time for celebration is the winter holiday season. Memories are made as families gather with friends to share food and enjoy each other's company. It's a time to reflect on the year gone by and to prepare for the year to come.

A bountiful table and the company of friends is what the Midwest is all about.

Although we strive with determination and creativity to achieve our goals, it always comes back to people. A belief in ourselves and each other has made ours an exemplary community from beginning to end.

The symphony is just one way we feed our love of the arts.

Shown left to right: Lemon Soufflé with Raspberry Sauce (pg. 183),
Rum Balls (pg. 211), Gourmet Strawberries (pg. 172),
Chocolate Walnut Bliss (pg. 101).

The winter holiday season is a time to reflect on the year gone by and prepare for the year ahead.

Shown left to right: Marinated Shrimp (pg. 55), Strawberry Glazed
Cheesecake (pg. 146), Cheese Triangles (pg. 43), Sauterne Clam
Puffs (pg. 29), Walnut Yule Log (pg. 102), English Trifle (pg. 174).

Desserts

Chocolate Rum Temptation Cake

Sinfully delicious!

Preparation: 45 minutes plus cooling time
Baking: 25-40 minutes as package directs
Yield: 10 servings

Ganache
1 cup heavy cream
4 ounces semi-sweet chocolate, finely chopped

- In heavy 2-quart saucepan, heat cream until simmering.
- Remove from heat and add chocolate.
- Pour into small bowl and refrigerate at least 2 hours.

Cake
1 box chocolate cake mix
2 large eggs
1 cup water
½ cup vegetable oil
½ cup dark rum

- Preheat oven to 350°.
- Grease and flour two 8-inch or 9-inch round cake pans.
- In large bowl, combine cake mix, eggs, water, oil and rum. Beat according to package directions.
- Pour batter into prepared pans and bake according to package directions.
- Cool cake layers on wire rack for 1 hour.

Filling
1 (3½ ounce) package "cook and serve" chocolate pudding mix
½ cup half-and-half
3 tablespoons dark rum
¼ cup crème fraîche or sour cream

- Combine pudding mix, half-and-half and rum in a 1½-quart saucepan and bring to a boil over medium high heat while stirring constantly.
- Simmer 1 minute or until thick.
- Cool to room temperature.
- Whisk in crème fraîche or sour cream.
- Refrigerate 1 hour or until cool.

Garnish
½ cup heavy cream
2 tablespoons powdered
sugar

- Just before assembling cake, combine cream and powdered sugar in large bowl and beat at high speed until stiff peaks form.
- Place in pastry bag with ½-inch star tip; set aside while assembling cake.

To Assemble:
- With electric mixer at medium high speed, beat ganache for 3-5 minutes or until thick enough to spread.
- Invert one cake layer onto serving platter.
- Spread filling on top.
- Place second layer on top of filling.
- With broad spatula, spread ganache over top and sides of cake.
- Pipe whipped cream onto cake. Refrigerate cake.
- Remove cake from refrigerator 30 minutes before serving.

Note: To make crème fraîche, combine 1 cup whipping cream and 1 tablespoon buttermilk. Stir well. Cover and let stand at slightly warm room temperature 10-12 hours or until thickened. Chill. This keeps in refrigerator 2 weeks.

French Chocolate Roll

This recipe is easier than it sounds and the rewards are incredible.

6 ounces semi-sweet chocolate
2 tablespoons strong coffee
1 teaspoon vanilla extract
6 eggs, separated
⅛ teaspoon salt
¾ cup sugar
3 tablespoons powdered sugar, divided
3 tablespoons unsweetened cocoa powder, divided
1 cup heavy cream

Preparation: 45 minutes plus overnight chilling
Baking: 16-18 minutes
Yield: 14 servings

- Preheat oven to 350°.
- Grease 15x10x1-inch jelly roll pan; line with wax paper, extending it a few inches at the narrow ends.
- Melt chocolate in coffee over low heat.
- Remove from heat; stir in vanilla until smooth and set aside to cool.
- In large bowl, beat egg whites with salt until soft peaks form.
- Add sugar, one tablespoon at a time, beating well until mixture forms stiff shiny peaks; set aside.
- Stir egg yolks to break up.
- Stir chocolate mixture into egg yolks until well blended.
- Fold ¼ of egg white mixture into chocolate mixture until well blended.
- Add to remaining egg whites; fold gently until blended.
- Pour into prepared pan and spread evenly.
- Bake 16-18 minutes or until top is firm.
- Remove from oven; run small knife around edges to loosen cake.
- Sift 2 tablespoons each of cocoa and powdered sugar onto clean towel.
- Invert pan onto coated towel.
- Working quickly, remove pan and peel wax paper; cool completely.
- Beat cream with remaining 1 tablespoon cocoa and powdered sugar until stiff.
- Spread over cake to within ½ inch of edges.
- Lift one side of towel until cake rolls inward; continue until cake is rolled. Roll will have cracks. Trim off ends.

- Transfer roll, carefully, seam side down, onto sheet of foil.
- Wrap foil firmly around roll and chill several hours or overnight.
- Remove foil; transfer to serving platter.
- Cut in 1-inch slices with sharp knife.
- Garnish with dollops of whipped cream and sprinkle with chocolate shavings.

Chocolate Walnut Bliss

Blissful!

Preparation: 25 minutes
Baking: 35 minutes
Yield: 10-12 servings

zest of large orange
1 cup sugar less one tablespoon
1 cup (6 ounces) chocolate chips
6 tablespoons butter or margarine
5 teaspoons orange or raspberry liqueur or orange juice
5 large eggs
2 cups finely chopped walnuts

- Preheat oven to 375°.
- Grease and flour 9-inch springform pan; line with wax paper.
- Grate zest of orange with sugar in food processor.
- Melt chocolate chips and butter.
- Stir sugar mixture into chocolate.
- Add liqueur or orange juice.
- Stir in eggs and nuts.
- Pour into prepared pan.
- Bake 35 minutes. Do not overbake.
- Cool 15 minutes; remove from pan.
- Cool completely on wire rack.

Glaze
1¼ cups chocolate chips
¼ cup butter
1½ tablespoons light corn syrup
walnut halves for garnish

- Melt chocolate and butter, stir until smooth.
- Add corn syrup; mix well.
- Pour glaze over cooled cake.
- Garnish with walnut halves.

Walnut Yule Log

This a very impressive holiday dessert. It keeps well in the refrigerator for several days and can be frozen.

Preparation: 30 minutes plus chilling and assembly
Baking: 12 minutes
Yield: 12 servings

Chocolate Roll

¾ **cup flour**
¼ **cup unsweetened cocoa powder**
1 **teaspoon baking powder**
¼ **teaspoon salt**
3 **eggs**
1 **cup sugar**
⅓ **cup water**
1 **teaspoon vanilla extract**
powdered sugar

- Preheat oven to 375°.
- Grease 15x10x1-inch jelly roll pan, line with wax paper, and grease again.
- Stir together flour, cocoa, baking powder and salt. Set aside.
- In small bowl, beat eggs about 5 minutes or until very thick and lemon colored.
- Pour eggs into large mixer bowl; gradually beat in sugar.
- On low speed, blend in water and vanilla.
- Gradually add flour mixture, beating just until batter is smooth.
- Pour into pan and spread to corners.
- Bake 12 minutes or until toothpick inserted in center comes out clean.
- Loosen cake from edges of pan. Invert on kitchen towel sprinkled with powdered sugar.
- Remove wax paper, trimming off cake edges if necessary.
- While cake is hot, roll cake and towel from narrow end.
- Cool completely.

Filling

2 egg yolks
2 tablespoons sugar
1 teaspoon cornstarch
½ cup light cream or half-and-half
¾ cup unsalted butter
1 cup powdered sugar
1 teaspoon dry instant coffee
1 teaspoon vanilla extract
1 cup very finely chopped walnuts

- Combine egg yolks, sugar and cornstarch in small saucepan. Blend in cream.
- Cook, stirring constantly, over medium heat, until mixture comes to a boil.
- Remove from heat. Cool. Chill.
- Beat butter in medium size bowl until soft and smooth.
- Beat in powdered sugar until smooth.
- Dissolve coffee in vanilla. Add to butter mixture.
- Gradually add chilled egg yolk mixture, 1 tablespoon at a time, while beating constantly.
- Beat until light and fluffy.
- Fold in nuts.

To assemble:
- Unroll cake carefully, spread with about ⅔ of walnut mixture.
- Roll, lifting cake with end of towel.
- Place seam side down on small cookie sheet.
- Spread remaining walnut mixture over roll.
- Chill overnight.
- When chilled, slice triangular shaped piece (1½-inches to 2-inches on long side) from end of roll.
- Place near top of roll toward one end, so it resembles a cut-off branch.

Glaze

¾ cup chocolate chips
3 tablespoons butter or margarine
1 tablespoon milk or cream

- Melt chocolate chips with butter and milk.
- Stir until smooth.
- Let stand about 5 minutes and then quickly spread over roll.
- Use a fork to make "bark-like" lines in glaze.
- Garnish with walnut halves or greenery.

Great Grandma's Dark Chocolate Cake

Very moist, deep dark chocolate.

Preparation: 20 minutes
Baking: 25-35 minutes
Yield: 12 servings

2 ounces bittersweet chocolate
½ cup shortening
1 cup water
2 cups flour, sifted
2 cups sugar
1½ teaspoons baking soda
½ teaspoon salt
2 eggs, well beaten
½ cup sour milk (1½ teaspoons vinegar plus enough milk to make ½ cup)
1 teaspoon vanilla extract

- Preheat oven to 350°.
- Grease and flour two 8-inch or 9-inch cake pans.
- Melt chocolate, shortening and water in a pan over low heat; stir and cool.
- Sift together flour, sugar, baking soda and salt.
- Blend cooled chocolate mixture with flour mixture.
- Add well-beaten eggs, sour milk and vanilla.
- Pour batter into prepared pans.
- Bake 25-35 minutes; cool.
- May be made in lined cupcake pans; bake 18-20 minutes.
- When cool, frost with Italian Butter Frosting.

Italian Butter Frosting

Light and fluffy. Not too sweet.

Preparation: 20 minutes plus chilling time
Yield: enough to frost a three-layer 8-inch cake

1½ cups milk
6 tablespoons flour
1½ cups butter or margarine
1½ cups sugar
1 tablespoon vanilla extract

- Blend milk and flour in saucepan until smooth.
- Cook over low heat until very thick, stirring constantly. It should be almost too thick to stir.
- Cool in refrigerator.
- Cream butter or margarine and sugar until light and fluffy.
- Add cooled flour mixture and beat until smooth.
- Add vanilla and blend well.
- Spread on cooled cake.

Flourless Chocolate Cake

A light flourless cake.

Preparation: 20 minutes
Baking: 35-45 minutes
Yield: 8-10 servings

**4¾ ounces bittersweet
   chocolate, chopped**
3 tablespoons unsalted butter
**4 eggs, separated, room
   temperature**
**3½ tablespoons sugar,
   divided**
1½ tablespoons brandy
¼ teaspoon cream of tartar
whipped cream
berries

- Preheat oven to 275°.
- Line 9-inch round cake pan with wax paper; butter paper.
- Melt chocolate and butter in top of double boiler over simmering water.
- Stir until smooth; remove from heat and set aside.
- Using electric mixer, beat egg yolks and 1¾ tablespoons sugar until doubled in volume and the consistency of whipped cream, about 5-8 minutes.
- Blend in brandy; fold in melted chocolate mixture.
- Using clean dry beaters, beat egg whites with cream of tartar until soft peaks form.
- Gradually add remaining 1¾ tablespoons sugar; beat until stiff but not dry.
- Fold into chocolate mixture.
- Pour batter into prepared pan and bake 35-45 minutes.
- Cool cake completely in pan.
- Place cake on serving platter; cut into slices.
- Serve with whipped cream and berries.

*Variation: ¾ cup semi-sweet chocolate chips
may be substituted for bittersweet chocolate.*

Turtle Cake

A favorite from Amish Acres in Nappanee, Indiana.

Preparation: 45 minutes
Baking: 40 minutes
Yield: 15-20 servings

1 (18 ounce) package German chocolate cake mix
1¼ cups water (or according to package directions)
⅓ cup vegetable oil (or according to package directions)
3 eggs (or according to package directions)
1 (14 ounce) package caramels, unwrapped
½ cup butter
7 ounces sweetened condensed milk
6 ounces pecans, chopped
1 cup (6 ounces) chocolate chips

- Preheat oven to 350°.
- Mix cake as directed on package.
- Pour half of cake batter into greased 9x13-inch baking pan.
- Bake 15 minutes or until done.
- In top of double boiler, melt together caramels, butter and milk. Stir until smooth.
- Remove from heat and cool slightly.
- Pour caramel mixture over partially baked cake.
- Pour remaining cake batter over caramels.
- Sprinkle with pecans and chocolate chips.
- Bake 25 minutes longer or until done.

Chocolate Cola Cake

A great kid's cake.

Preparation: 30 minutes
Baking: 30 minutes
Yield: 15 servings

1 cup margarine
¼ cup unsweetened cocoa
   powder
1 cup cola
2 cups flour
2 cups sugar
1 teaspoon baking soda
½ cup buttermilk
2 eggs, beaten
1 teaspoon vanilla extract
1½ cups mini-marshmallows

- Preheat oven to 350°.
- In a medium saucepan, combine margarine, cocoa and cola; heat to boiling.
- Add flour, sugar and baking soda; mix gently.
- Stir in buttermilk, eggs, vanilla and marshmallows until melted.
- Pour into greased 9x13-inch baking pan.
- Bake 30 minutes.
- Frost cake while still warm.

Chocolate Marshmallow Frosting

½ cup margarine
¼ cup unsweetened cocoa
   powder
2 tablespoons cola
1 cup mini-marshmallows
4 cups powdered sugar
1 teaspoon vanilla extract
1 cup chopped pecans

- Combine margarine, cocoa and cola and heat to boiling.
- Add marshmallows, stirring until melted.
- Beat in sugar and vanilla; stir in nuts.
- Spread on warm cake.

Black Bottom Cupcakes

Kids will love these.

Preparation: 30 minutes
Baking: 30 minutes
Yield: 24 servings

Filling
**8 ounces cream cheese,
    softened**
1 egg
⅓ cup sugar
⅛ teaspoon salt
**1 cup (6 ounces) semi-sweet
    chocolate chips**

- Preheat oven to 350°.
- In a medium bowl, combine cream cheese, egg, ⅓ cup sugar, and ⅛ teaspoon salt.
- Beat well. Stir in chocolate chips. Set aside.

Batter
1½ cups flour
1 cup sugar
**¼ cup unsweetened cocoa
    powder**
1 teaspoon baking soda
½ teaspoon salt
1 cup water
⅓ cup vegetable oil
1 tablespoon white vinegar
1 teaspoon vanilla extract
2 tablespoons sugar
⅓ cup chopped walnuts

- In a large bowl, mix together flour, 1 cup sugar, cocoa, baking soda, and ½ teaspoon salt.
- Stir in water, oil, vinegar, and vanilla. Beat well.
- Line muffin tins with cupcake papers. Fill each ⅓ full with chocolate batter.
- Top each cupcake with a heaping teaspoon of cream cheese filling.
- Sprinkle with sugar and nuts.
- Bake 25-30 minutes. Do not overbake. Cool at least 4 hours.

*Variation: These cupcakes may be made in
greased mini-muffin tins. The yield will be approximately
72 mini-cupcakes, and baking time will be about 12 minutes.*

Fudge Cake

An old family recipe that always gets raves!

Preparation: 15 minutes
Baking: 45-55 minutes
Yield: 12-15 servings

⅔ cup vegetable oil
4 ounces unsweetened
   chocolate, melted
2 eggs
2 cups sugar
2½ cups flour
1 teaspoon baking soda
1 teaspoon salt
1 teaspoon vanilla extract
1½ cups water
1 cup (6 ounces) chocolate
   chips
¾ cup chopped nuts

- Preheat oven to 350°.
- Combine oil, chocolate, eggs, sugar, flour, baking soda, salt, vanilla and water.
- Pour into greased 9x13-inch baking pan.
- Sprinkle chocolate chips and nuts on top.
- Bake 45-55 minutes or until toothpick comes out clean.
- Cool cake and frost.

Fluffy Frosting
½ cup margarine, softened
½ cup shortening
1 cup sugar
½ cup scalded milk
1 teaspoon vanilla extract

- Beat margarine, shortening and sugar until light and fluffy, at least 3 minutes.
- Slowly add hot milk and vanilla and beat again until light and fluffy.
- Spread on cooled cake.

Devil Dogs

Great alternative to cupcakes for children's parties. Adults love them, too!

Preparation: 30 minutes plus assembly
Baking: 6-8 minutes
Yield: 18-20 cakes

Cake

½ cup unsweetened cocoa
  powder
1 cup sugar
1 egg
½ cup shortening
1 teaspoon vanilla extract
1 cup milk
1½ teaspoons baking soda
½ teaspoon baking powder
½ teaspoon salt
2 cups flour

- Preheat oven to 400°.
- Combine all cake ingredients and mix well.
- Drop dough by teaspoonfuls onto ungreased cookie sheets.
- Bake 6-8 minutes; let cool.

Filling

¾ cup butter or margarine,
  softened
1⅔ cups powdered sugar
½ teaspoon vanilla extract
1 (7 ounce) jar marshmallow
  creme

- Cream butter and powdered sugar.
- Add vanilla and marshmallow creme; beat well.
- Arrange cooled cakes in pairs of equal size.
- Place filling on one cake of each pair to a thickness of about ⅛ inch; top with second cake.

Almond Meringue Torte

Elegant and colorful!

Preparation: 45 minutes
Baking: 30 minutes
Yield: 12 servings

½ cup sugar
½ cup shortening
4 large eggs, separated
3 tablespoons milk
1 teaspoon vanilla extract
1 cup cake flour
1 teaspoon baking powder
¼ teaspoon salt
pinch of salt
pinch of cream of tartar
¾ cup sugar
½ cup sliced almonds,
    toasted
1 tablespoon sugar
½ teaspoon cinnamon
1 cup whipping cream
2 teaspoons sugar
1 teaspoon vanilla extract
fresh fruit: strawberries,
    raspberries, blueberries,
    kiwi

- Preheat oven to 350°.
- In a mixing bowl, cream ½ cup sugar and shortening.
- Add egg yolks, one at a time, beating well after each addition.
- Stir in milk and 1 teaspoon vanilla.
- Combine flour, baking powder and ¼ teaspoon salt.
- Add to creamed mixture and beat until smooth.
- Pour into 2 greased 9-inch cake pans.
- Beat egg whites with pinch of salt and pinch of cream of tartar until soft peaks form.
- Beat in ¾ cup sugar, 1 tablespoon at a time until glossy and stiff peaks form.
- Spread meringue evenly over batter, dividing meringue between the two pans.
- Sprinkle with almonds and 1 tablespoon sugar mixed with cinnamon.
- Bake 30 minutes. Turn out onto racks.
- Using second rack, turn again so meringue is right side up. Cool.
- Save any almonds that fall off for garnish.
- Just before assembling, whip cream and sweeten with 2 teaspoons sugar and 1 teaspoon vanilla.
- No more than 6 hours before serving, place one layer on serving plate, meringue side up.
- Spread with ¾ of the whipping cream and fruit.
- Top with remaining layer, meringue side up.
- Garnish with remaining whipping cream and fruit.

Chocolate Truffle Torte

This involves dirtying several bowls but it is not as difficult as it may appear. Beautiful striped effect when sliced.

Preparation: 1 hour and 10 minutes plus chilling
Baking: 30 minutes
Yield: 16-20 servings

Cake
1 box Devil's Food cake mix
1¼ cups water (or as package directs)
3 eggs
⅓-½ cup oil or butter (or as package directs)

• Preheat oven according to package instructions.
• Prepare cake according to package directions.
• Bake in 3 greased and floured 8-inch or 9-inch cake pans, 20-30 minutes, or until done.
• Remove from pans and cool completely.

Truffle Filling
1 cup (6 ounces) semi-sweet chocolate chips
4 tablespoons butter, cut into pieces
½ cup whipping cream
¼ cup sugar

• Heat everything together in saucepan, stirring until completely melted and smooth. Do not overheat. Set aside.

Whipped Cream Filling
2 cups whipping cream
¼ cup powdered sugar
2 teaspoons vanilla extract
⅓-½ cup crème de cacao
3 tablespoons water
1 envelope unflavored gelatin

• Beat cream until it begins to thicken.
• Add powdered sugar, vanilla and crème de cacao and beat until stiff. Do not overbeat.
• Set aside for 10 minutes to lose some of its chill.
• Put water and gelatin in glass measuring cup. Soften 1 minute then heat in microwave until gelatin dissolves (less than 1 minute). Cool 2-3 minutes.
• Beat or whisk gelatin mixture into whipped cream mixture, working quickly so that gelatin does not set.

To Assemble:

• Place pan of chocolate truffle filling in large bowl of ice water and stir until consistency of peanut butter. Remove from ice water.

• Slice each cake layer in half horizontally.

• Put first half-layer of cake on plate, spread with ⅓ of the whipped cream mixture.

• Add next half-layer, spread with ½ chocolate truffle filling.

• Continue assembling cake, alternating whipped cream and chocolate truffle filling.

• Wrap well in plastic and refrigerate at least 2 hours. Keeps very well 3-4 days at this stage.

Cake Frosting

1 cup whipping cream
2 tablespoons powdered sugar
1 teaspoon vanilla extract

• Three to six hours before serving, whip cream until beginning to thicken.

• Add powdered sugar and vanilla; beat until thick and stiff. Do not overbeat or frosting will not spread smoothly.

• Frost top and sides of cake; refrigerate.

• Garnish with chocolate curls, strawberries, or fresh flowers.

Heath Bar Meringue

This will get raves.

Preparation: 40 minutes plus chilling
Baking: 1½ hours
Yield: 6-8 servings

Meringue Crust
3 egg whites
½ teaspoon baking powder
⅛ teaspoon salt
1 teaspoon vanilla extract
1 teaspoon vinegar
1 teaspoon water
1 cup sugar

- Preheat oven to 275°.
- In a medium bowl, combine all ingredients except sugar and beat well.
- Add sugar, 1 tablespoon at a time. Beat 2 more minutes after all sugar has been added.
- Grease and flour two 8-inch round cake pans.
- Pour meringue evenly into prepared pans. Bake for 1½ hours.

Filling
1 cup whipping cream
3 Heath bars, chopped
½ cup chopped pecans

- In a medium bowl, whip cream until stiff.
- Add Heath bars and pecans.
- Place 1 meringue on a serving plate. Spread with ½ whipping cream mixture.
- Layer remaining meringue and then whipping cream.
- Refrigerate overnight.
- Garnish with fresh fruit or chocolate curls.

Raspberry Walnut Torte and Sauce

Out of this world!

Preparation: 45 minutes
Baking: 1 hour
Yield: 15 servings

1¼ cups flour, divided
⅓ cup powdered sugar
½ cup butter, softened
2 (10 ounce) packages frozen raspberries in light syrup, thawed
¾ cup chopped walnuts
2 eggs
1 cup sugar
½ teaspoon salt
½ teaspoon baking powder
1 teaspoon vanilla extract
whipped cream or ice cream

- Preheat oven to 350°.
- Combine 1 cup flour, powdered sugar and butter; blend well.
- Press mixture into bottom of 9x13-inch baking pan.
- Bake 15 minutes. Cool.
- Drain raspberries and reserve liquid for sauce.
- Spoon berries over crust. Sprinkle walnuts on top.
- Beat eggs with sugar until light and fluffy.
- Add salt, ¼ cup flour, baking powder and vanilla; blend well.
- Pour over walnuts.
- Bake 30-35 minutes or until golden brown.
- Cool and cut into squares. Serve with whipped cream and sauce.

Raspberry Sauce

½ cup water
reserved raspberry juice
½ cup sugar
2 tablespoons cornstarch
1 tablespoon lemon juice

- Combine water, raspberry juice, sugar and cornstarch.
- Cook, stirring constantly, until thick and clear.
- Stir in lemon juice.
- Cool.

Hazelnut Torte

This is a swell cake—very nice doubled to four layers.

Preparation: *30 minutes*
Baking: *20 minutes*
Yield: *12 servings*

2 tablespoons flour
2½ teaspoons baking powder
4 eggs
¾ cup sugar
1 cup hazelnuts

- Preheat oven to 350°.
- Prepare two 8-inch cake pans by greasing, lining with wax paper, and greasing paper.
- Sift flour and baking powder together; set aside.
- Put eggs and sugar into blender; cover and process on low until smooth.
- Turn to high and add nuts gradually, processing until they are fine.
- Add flour mixture all at once, processing only until mixed.
- Pour into prepared pans.
- Bake 20 minutes.
- Invert cake layers onto wire racks.
- Remove wax paper. Brush on glaze.

Glaze
¼ cup sugar
1½ tablespoons water
1½ tablespoons hazelnut liqueur

- While cake is baking, combine sugar and water in pan. Simmer 2 minutes, just until sugar dissolves.
- Cool and add liqueur.
- Brush on warm cake layers.
- If desired, layers can now be wrapped and frozen.
- Frost room temperature cake with Cream Cheese Whipped Cream Frosting.

Cream Cheese Whipped Cream Frosting

1 teaspoon unflavored gelatin
1½ tablespoons water
4 ounces cream cheese, room temperature
3 tablespoons powdered sugar
½ teaspoon vanilla extract
1½ cups whipping cream
½ cup hazelnuts, toasted and finely chopped

- In small bowl, sprinkle gelatin over water. Let soften for 1 minute.
- Place bowl over simmering water and stir to dissolve gelatin.
- Beat together room temperature cream cheese, gelatin mixture, powdered sugar and vanilla.
- Gradually beat in cream until soft peaks form.
- Use to frost between layers, top and sides of cake.
- Sprinkle with chopped hazelnuts.
- Refrigerate until ready to serve. Can be stored up to 2 days.

Variation: Almonds can be substituted for the hazelnuts. Use an almond-flavored liqueur in the glaze.

Note: Hazelnuts can often be located at natural food stores.

Frozen Chocolate Torte

Worth every calorie!

Preparation: 30 minutes plus freezing
Baking: 1 ½ hours
Yield: 8-10 servings

3 egg whites
½ teaspoon cream of tartar
¾ cup sugar
½ cup chopped pecans
2 cups whipping cream
½ teaspoon vanilla extract
¾ cup chocolate syrup, room temperature

- Preheat oven to 275°.
- Beat egg whites until frothy.
- Add cream of tartar. Beat until soft peaks form.
- Add sugar, 1 tablespoon at a time, beating until stiff.
- Fold in pecans.
- Draw two 8-inch circles on parchment paper. Place parchment on baking sheets.
- Spread meringue evenly over each circle.
- Bake 45 minutes.
- Turn oven off. Leave meringue in oven an additional 45 minutes with door closed.
- Whip the cream in a chilled bowl with chilled beaters, beating until stiff.
- Gently fold in vanilla and chocolate syrup.
- Place one meringue layer on serving plate. Spread with ½ of the chocolate mixture. Top with second meringue and then remaining chocolate.
- Place in freezer for 4 hours or overnight.

Italian Creme Cake

Superb!

Preparation: 20 minutes
Baking: 25-30 minutes
Yield: 12-14 servings

½ cup butter, softened
½ cup shortening
2 cups sugar
5 eggs, separated
1 teaspoon vanilla extract
1 teaspoon baking soda
1 cup buttermilk
2 cups flour, sifted
4 teaspoons cream of tartar
1 cup coconut
1 cup chopped pecans

- Preheat oven to 350°.
- Grease and flour three 8-inch cake pans.
- Cream together butter, shortening and sugar.
- Add egg yolks, one at a time, beating well; add vanilla.
- Combine baking soda and buttermilk.
- Add to creamed mixture alternately with flour and cream of tartar.
- Stir in coconut and pecans.
- Beat egg whites; fold into mixture.
- Divide batter evenly among prepared pans.
- Bake 25-30 minutes.
- Frost when cool.

Frosting

8 ounces cream cheese, softened
½ cup butter, softened
4 cups powdered sugar
1 teaspoon vanilla extract
chopped pecans

- Combine cream cheese, butter, powdered sugar and vanilla and beat until smooth.
- Blend in nuts.
- Frost cooled cake.

Margaret's Apple Cake

Keeps well for several days if it lasts that long!

Preparation: 1 hour
Baking: 45-60 minutes
Yield: 16-20 servings

4 cups tart apples, peeled and coarsely chopped (approximately 3 pounds)
2 cups sugar
2 eggs
½ cup vegetable oil
2 teaspoons vanilla extract
2 cups flour
2 teaspoons baking soda
2 teaspoons cinnamon
½ teaspoon salt
1 cup coarsely chopped walnuts

- Preheat oven to 350°.
- Grease and flour 9x13-inch baking pan.
- Cover chopped apples with sugar. Let stand until ready to use.
- Beat eggs slightly; add oil and vanilla. Beat well.
- Sift together flour, baking soda, cinnamon and salt.
- Add dry ingredients alternately with apples to egg mixture.
- Add chopped walnuts.
- Spread into prepared pan.
- Bake 45-60 minutes. Cool and frost.

Lemony Butter Frosting

½ cup butter, softened
3 cups powdered sugar
2 tablespoons lemon juice

- Cream butter until fluffy.
- Add powdered sugar; beat until smooth.
- Add lemon juice and mix until frosting is of spreading consistency.

No-Egg Applesauce Cake

This cake may be topped with whipped cream for a fancy dessert or served plain as a snack cake.

Preparation: 15 minutes
Baking: 45-50 minutes
Yield: 6 large or 12 small pieces

2 cups flour
1 cup sugar
1 teaspoon salt
1 teaspoon cinnamon
½ teaspoon nutmeg
¼ teaspoon ground cloves
2 teaspoons baking soda
1 cup raisins
1 cup chopped walnuts
½ cup butter, melted
2 cups applesauce

- Preheat oven to 350°.
- Grease and flour 9-inch square pan or 8x12-inch baking pan.
- Sift all dry ingredients together.
- Add remaining ingredients and beat until well blended.
- Pour into prepared pan.
- Bake 45-50 minutes.
- Cool before cutting.

14 Carat Cake

*This "carat" cake really
sparkles!*

Preparation: 20 minutes
Baking: 25-30 minutes
Yield: 12 servings

2 cups sugar
2 cups flour
2 teaspoons baking soda
2 teaspoons cinnamon
1 scant teaspoon salt
4 eggs
1½ cups vegetable oil
3 cups grated carrots (about
** 8 medium carrots)**

- Preheat oven to 350°.
- Grease three 8-inch round cake pans and line each with wax paper.
- Mix dry ingredients together.
- Add eggs one at a time, alternating with oil. Mix well after each addition.
- Stir in carrots.
- Pour into prepared pans.
- Bake 25-30 minutes.
- Cool and frost tops of each layer with Maple Cream Frosting. Garnish with pecans.

Maple Cream Frosting

*This frosting will make any cake
exceptional.*

Preparation: 15 minutes
Yield: will frost three 8-inch cake layers

1 pound cream cheese,
** softened**
½ cup maple syrup
1 cup heavy cream, whipped

- Combine cream cheese and maple syrup and blend well.
- Gently fold whipped cream into cream cheese mixture until well blended.

Easy Carrot Cake

*Quick and easy—no grating
necessary.*

*Preparation: 15 minutes
Baking: 50 minutes
Yield: 15-20 servings*

1 cup vegetable oil
2 cups flour
3 eggs
2 cups sugar
2 teaspoons baking powder
2 teaspoons cinnamon
2 teaspoons vanilla extract
**2 (7½ ounce) jars junior baby
   carrots (from baby food
   section)**
1 cup chopped pecans
**1 (8 ounce) can crushed
   pineapple, drained**

- Preheat oven to 350°.
- Grease and flour 9x13-inch baking pan.
- Combine all ingredients; mix by hand.
- Pour into prepared pan and bake 50 minutes.
- Frost when cool.

Cream Cheese Frosting

**8 ounces cream cheese,
   softened**
½ cup butter, softened
1 cup chopped pecans
1 teaspoon vanilla extract
4 cups powdered sugar

- Combine all ingredients and mix until smooth.
- Spread on cooled cake.

Upside-Down Peach Gingerbread

*Wonderful for brunch or
luncheon.*

*Preparation: 15 minutes
Baking: 30-40 minutes
Yield: 8-10 servings*

¾ **cup margarine, divided**
1¼ **cups firmly packed brown
    sugar, divided**
5 **peaches, peeled and sliced**
½ **cup chopped pecans**
¼ **teaspoon grated lemon
    rind**
1 **egg**
¼ **cup molasses**
1¼ **cups flour**
1¼ **teaspoons ground ginger**
¾ **teaspoon cinnamon**
½ **teaspoon baking soda**
¼ **teaspoon salt**
¼ **teaspoon nutmeg**
⅛ **teaspoon ground cloves**
⅓ **cup boiling water**

- Preheat oven to 350°.
- Melt ¼ cup margarine in 9-inch round cake pan; add ¾ cup brown sugar.
- Place in oven and cook until sugar begins to melt; remove from oven.
- Arrange peaches and pecans on top; sprinkle with lemon rind.
- Cream ½ cup margarine and ½ cup brown sugar in a mixing bowl.
- Beat in egg and molasses.
- Mix together flour, ginger, cinnamon, baking soda, salt, nutmeg and ground cloves.
- Stir into creamed mixture and pour in water.
- Beat just until all ingredients are mixed; do not overbeat.
- Spoon mixture evenly over peaches.
- Bake 30-40 minutes.
- Let cool 5 minutes.
- Invert carefully onto serving platter and serve warm.

Pear Upside-Down Spice Cake

Deserves your best cake plate.

Preparation: 30 minutes
Baking: 40-45 minutes
Yield: 8-10 servings

3 tablespoons margarine
⅔ cup firmly packed brown sugar
1 (29 ounce) can pear halves
1 cup chopped walnuts
⅓ cup margarine, softened
½ cup sugar
1 egg
1¼ cups flour
1½ teaspoons baking powder
1 teaspoon baking soda
½ teaspoon salt
½ teaspoon cinnamon
½ teaspoon nutmeg
¼ teaspoon ground cloves

- Preheat oven to 350°.
- Melt margarine in 9-inch cake pan in preheated oven.
- Add brown sugar and place in oven until sugar begins to melt.
- Remove from oven.
- Slice each pear half into 5 fan-like pieces.
- Arrange pears on top of brown sugar mixture.
- Sprinkle walnuts on top of pears.
- Cream margarine, sugar and egg in mixing bowl.
- Combine flour, baking powder, soda, salt, cinnamon, nutmeg and ground cloves.
- Stir into creamed mixture and spoon evenly over pears.
- Bake 40-45 minutes.
- Cool slightly.
- Invert carefully and serve while slightly warm.

Variation: Canned peach halves may be substituted for the pear halves.

Chocolate Zucchini Loaf

You'll never know the zucchini's in there!

Preparation: 30 minutes
Baking: 50-60 minutes
Freezes very well
Yield: 2 large or 4 small loaves

4 eggs
3 cups sugar
1½ cups vegetable oil
3 ounces unsweetened
   chocolate, melted
3 cups flour
1½ teaspoons baking powder
1 teaspoon baking soda
1 teaspoon salt
3 cups shredded zucchini
   (about 1¼ pounds)
1 cup chopped nuts
2 cups (12 ounces) semi-
   sweet chocolate chips

- Preheat oven to 350°.
- Grease and flour two 9x5-inch loaf pans.
- Beat eggs until thick and light colored.
- Add sugar gradually, beating well.
- Add oil and melted chocolate; beat well.
- Mix dry ingredients together in separate bowl.
- Add dry ingredients to chocolate mixture alternately with zucchini, stirring by hand if necessary.
- Stir in nuts and chocolate chips.
- Pour into prepared loaf pans.
- Bake 50-60 minutes.
- Let stand in pans on racks 10 minutes.
- Remove from pans and cool.
- Slices better after 24 hours.

Note: Can be prepared in four 3x4-inch loaf pans
for gift giving. Bake 35-40 minutes.

Swedish Pineapple Cake

Great take-along cake.

Preparation: 10 minutes
Baking: 40-45 minutes
Yield: 15-20 servings

2 cups flour
2 cups sugar
1 teaspoon baking soda
1 (16 ounce) can crushed
  pineapple, undrained
2 eggs, beaten
1 teaspoon vanilla extract
½ cup chopped nuts

- Preheat oven to 350°.
- Sift together flour, sugar and baking soda.
- Add pineapple, eggs, vanilla and nuts. Mix well.
- Bake 40-45 minutes in well greased 9x13-inch baking pan.
- Cool and frost.

Cream Cheese Frosting
8 ounces cream cheese,
  softened
½ cup margarine, softened
1½ cups powdered sugar
1 teaspoon vanilla extract
½ cup chopped nuts

- Blend cream cheese and margarine together.
- Add powdered sugar and vanilla. Beat until smooth.
- Stir in nuts and frost cooled cake.

Apricot Cream Cake

This cake tastes best when served at room temperature.

Preparation: 30 minutes
Baking: 50-55 minutes
Yield: 14 servings

Cake
1 box butter flavor or yellow
  cake mix
¾ cup apricot nectar (in
  canned juice section)
¼ cup butter or margarine,
  softened
3 eggs

- Preheat oven to 350°.
- Grease and flour 10-inch Bundt pan or tube pan.
- In a large bowl, combine cake mix, apricot nectar, butter and eggs.
- Beat as directed on package. Do not underbeat.
- Spoon batter into prepared pan.

Filling
1 pound cream cheese,
  softened
½ cup sugar
2 tablespoons lemon juice
1 cup flaked coconut

- Combine filling ingredients in small bowl; beat until smooth.
- Spoon filling over batter in pan, being careful not to let it touch sides of pan.
- Bake 50-55 minutes or until top springs back when lightly pressed.
- Cool in pan at least 1 hour; remove from pan.
- Glaze when completely cooled.

Glaze
2 cups powdered sugar
2 tablespoons lemon juice
2 tablespoons apricot nectar

- Combine ingredients and mix until smooth.
- Drizzle over cooled cake.
- Store cake in refrigerator.

Blueberry Cake

Delightful with raspberries, too!

Preparation: 30 minutes
Baking: 70 minutes
Yield: 12 servings

1½ cups unsalted butter,
  softened
1½ cups sugar
4 eggs
1 teaspoon vanilla extract
1½ cups flour
1 teaspoon baking powder
1 pint blueberries
powdered sugar

- Preheat oven to 350°.
- Grease and flour 9-inch springform pan.
- Cream butter and sugar until light and fluffy.
- Add eggs, one at a time, beating after each addition.
- Add vanilla.
- Sift together flour and baking powder.
- Gradually add flour mixture to creamed butter mixture.
- Beat for a moment at high speed to make it fluffy.
- Fold in blueberries.
- Pour into prepared pan.
- Bake 70 minutes.
- Dust with powdered sugar after cooled.

Lemon Pound Cake

This is great served with strawberries and whipped cream!

Preparation: 15 minutes
Baking: 1 hour
Freezes well up to 3 months
Yield: 20 servings

1 cup butter, softened
½ cup shortening
4 eggs
2¾ cups sugar
3 cups flour
¼ teaspoon baking soda
½ teaspoon salt
1 cup buttermilk
1 teaspoon vanilla extract
2 teaspoons lemon extract
1 teaspoon lemon peel

- Preheat oven to 350°.
- Beat butter and shortening until light and fluffy.
- Add 1 egg alternately with about ¾ cup sugar until all eggs and sugar are used.
- Beat until fluffy.
- Stir together flour, baking soda and salt.
- Add alternately with buttermilk to butter mixture.
- Mix in vanilla, lemon extract and lemon peel.
- Pour into 2 greased 8x4-inch loaf pans.
- Bake 1 hour or until a toothpick inserted in center comes out clean.

Cream Cheese Pound Cake

Great alone or with a variety of sauces.

Preparation: 25 minutes
Baking: 1 hour and 10 minutes
Freezes well when tightly wrapped
Yield: 10-12 servings

¾ cup margarine, softened
8 ounces cream cheese, softened
1½ cups sugar
1½ teaspoons vanilla extract
4 eggs
2 cups sifted cake flour
1½ teaspoons baking powder
powdered sugar

- Preheat oven to 325°.
- Thoroughly blend margarine, cream cheese, sugar and vanilla.
- Add eggs, one at a time, beating well after each addition.
- Gradually add flour sifted with baking powder.
- Pour into greased 9x5-inch loaf pan.
- Bake 1 hour and 10 minutes.
- Let stand 5 minutes. Remove from pan and cool on wire rack.
- Sprinkle with powdered sugar.

Lemon Sauce

Wonderful on vanilla ice cream or angel food cake.

Preparation: 10 minutes
Yield: 1 ½ cups

1 tablespoon flour
1 cup sugar
¼ teaspoon salt
3 eggs, well-beaten
1 cup boiling water
grated rind of 1 lemon
juice of 2 lemons

- Combine flour, sugar and salt in a medium saucepan.
- Add eggs to dry ingredients.
- Add boiling water gradually, stirring constantly until smooth.
- Add rind and juice.
- Cook over medium-low heat, stirring constantly, until thickened.

Blueberry Sauce

A sweet, tart topping with a rich purple color.

Preparation: 20 minutes
Yield: ¾ cup

1 cup blueberries
½ cup water
¾ cup sugar
2 tablespoons cornstarch
1 tablespoon lemon juice

- Combine blueberries and water in saucepan.
- Heat just to boiling.
- Reduce heat and simmer 2 minutes.
- Strain, reserving ½ cup of juice.
- Combine sugar and cornstarch in saucepan.
- Gradually add reserved juice.
- Cook, stirring constantly, until thick and clear.
- Cool slightly and add lemon juice.
- Serve over cheesecake or pound cake.
- This sauce may be kept in a tightly sealed container in refrigerator for up to 3 weeks.

Apple Strudel

Recipe may be halved but then there won't be as much to enjoy!

Preparation: 1 hour
Baking: 30 minutes
Yield: 5-6 strudels, 50-60 pieces

10-15 apples
sugar, cinnamon and lemon
juice
½-1 cup raisins
1½-2 cups finely ground nuts
1½-2 cups fine dry bread
crumbs
½-1 pound butter, melted
1 pound phyllo dough,
thawed as package directs
powdered sugar

- Preheat oven to 350°.
- Peel, core and slice apples. Sprinkle with lemon juice. Sweeten with sugar and cinnamon to taste.
- Add raisins; mix well.
- Stack 4 sheets phyllo dough on dampened pillowcase or non-terry dishtowel. Keep remainder covered and refrigerated.
- Fold sheets in half, resembling a book. Open 1st page, brush with melted butter and sprinkle lightly with nuts and bread crumbs.
- Repeat with 2nd and 3rd pages.
- Flip book over to back. Open back page, brush with melted butter and sprinkle with nuts and bread crumbs. Repeat with 2nd and 3rd pages, then middle page.
- Using slotted spoon, place some apple filling along side nearest you. Roll up like a jelly roll, using pillowcase as an aid. Tuck ends in.
- Brush with melted butter, place on buttered baking sheet and refrigerate.
- Repeat with remaining phyllo dough and filling.
- With serrated knife, score each strudel lightly into serving pieces.
- Bake 10 minutes.

- Cut through serving pieces, push back together and brush with butter.
- Bake 10 minutes longer. Brush with butter.
- Bake 10 minutes longer or until lightly browned.
- Let cool and sprinkle with powdered sugar.
- Strudels may be prepared and frozen before baking. Thaw partially before baking as directed above. They may also be frozen after baking. To serve, recrisp in 350° oven, partially covered, for 10 minutes.

Cranberry Streusel Cake

Great for the holidays. Topping tastes like cranberry sauce!

Preparation: 20 minutes
Baking: 55 minutes
Yield: 10-12 servings

1½ cups margarine, softened
1 cup sugar
4 eggs
1 teaspoon vanilla extract
1¾ cups flour
2 teaspoons baking powder
2 cups whole fresh cranberries
¼ cup flour
½ cup firmly packed light brown sugar
1 teaspoon cinnamon
2 tablespoons margarine
¼ cup chopped pecans

- Preheat oven to 350°.
- Grease and flour 9-inch springform pan.
- Cream 1½ cups margarine and sugar with electric mixer until fluffy.
- Add eggs one at a time, beating after each addition.
- Add vanilla.
- Stir flour and baking powder together.
- Gradually add dry ingredients to sugar mixture.
- Beat for 1 minute on high speed.
- Place cake mixture in prepared pan.
- Place cranberries on top of batter.
- Mix together flour, brown sugar, cinnamon and margarine.
- Add pecans.
- Sprinkle on top of cranberries.
- Bake 55 minutes or until toothpick inserted in center comes out clean.

Cheese Strudel

This could become a family tradition.

Preparation: 30 minutes
Baking: 30-40 minutes
Freezes well before baking
Yield: 2 strudels

Pastry Dough
2 cups flour
1 cup butter
1 cup (8 ounces) sour cream

- In a medium bowl, cut butter into flour.
- Add sour cream. Mix thoroughly with electric mixer. Mix with hands if necessary.
- Divide dough in half and form 2 balls.
- Cover with wax paper. Refrigerate while preparing filling.

Filling
1 pound cream cheese, softened
½ cup sugar
1 teaspoon vanilla extract
1 egg

- Preheat oven to 350°.
- In a medium bowl, combine all ingredients. Mix until creamy.
- Roll out one ball of dough on a lightly floured board until very thin and in the shape of an oval (about 15x20-inches).
- Fold dough to transfer to a cookie sheet. Unfold dough on cookie sheet, allowing edges to hang over the pan.
- Place half of filling in center of dough. Spread filling lengthwise on dough into a 6x16-inch rectangle.
- There should be enough dough on either side to overlap on top of filling.
- Fold sides of pastry to the center, overlapping dough.
- Fold up the ends. Prick top of strudel with a fork.
- Repeat with second ball of dough and remaining filling.
- Bake for 30-40 minutes or until golden brown. Cool.
- When cool, glaze as directed on following page.

Glaze

¼ cup powdered sugar
few drops of water

- Mix powdered sugar and water to make a thin frosting.
- Drizzle over cooled strudels.

Freezing Information: The strudels may be frozen individually before baking. Freeze on cookie sheet. Remove and wrap in aluminum foil. To bake, unwrap, place on cookie sheet, and bake at 350° for 45 minutes.

Pluckets

Also makes a great after-school snack for kids.

Preparation: 45 minutes plus rising time
Baking: 40 minutes
Yield: 10-12 servings

1 package yeast
¼ cup warm water
⅓ cup butter, melted
⅓ cup sugar
½ teaspoon salt
1 cup scalded milk
3 eggs, beaten
4 cups flour
1 cup walnuts, chopped
6 tablespoons cinnamon
1 cup sugar
1 cup butter, melted

- Dissolve yeast in warm water.
- Add ⅓ cup butter, ⅓ cup sugar and salt to scalded milk and stir.
- When mixture has cooled to lukewarm, add dissolved yeast, eggs and flour and beat thoroughly.
- Cover with cloth and let rise until dough is doubled, about 2 hours.
- Stir dough down, cover and let rise until doubled again, another 1-2 hours.
- Preheat oven to 400°.
- Mix together walnuts, cinnamon and 1 cup sugar.
- Take 1 teaspoon of dough and dip into 1 cup melted butter, then into cinnamon sugar mixture.
- Pile balls loosely in ungreased angel food cake pan.
- Let rise 30 minutes.
- Pour any remaining butter and/or cinnamon sugar mixture over top.
- Bake at 400° for 10 minutes, then at 350° for 30 minutes.
- Remove from oven and turn upside down onto serving plate immediately.
- Serve warm and eat as bite-size "pluckets".

Poppy Seed Pound Cake

Rich pound cake with a twist.

Preparation: 20 minutes
Baking: 75-90 minutes
Yield: 12-16 servings

1 cup butter, softened
3 cups sugar
6 eggs
3 cups flour
1 cup heavy cream
¼ cup poppy seeds
1 tablespoon vanilla extract

- Grease and flour tube pan.
- Cream butter and sugar.
- Add eggs one at a time, beating well after each addition. Continue to beat 3 minutes.
- Gently fold in flour and heavy cream alternately.
- Add poppy seeds and vanilla.
- Pour into prepared pan.
- Place in cold oven.
- Heat oven to 325°.
- Bake 75-90 minutes.
- Cool before serving.

Triple Chocolate Cheesecake

It's gooey, rich, and chocolaty.

Preparation: 30 minutes
Baking: 50 minutes
Yield: 12-14 servings

Crust

½ cup lightly salted butter,
    melted
2 cups finely crushed
    chocolate wafers
¼ cup sugar

- Combine butter, crumbs and sugar until well blended.
- Press mixture into bottom and sides of 10-inch springform pan.

Filling

2 pounds cream cheese,
    softened
1¼ cups sugar
1 tablespoon light rum
1½ teaspoons vanilla extract
3½ ounces German sweet
    chocolate, melted
4 large eggs
½ cup mini chocolate chips

- Preheat oven to 350°.
- Combine cream cheese and sugar. Beat 2 minutes.
- Add rum, vanilla, and melted chocolate. Blend thoroughly.
- Add eggs, one at a time, beating on low speed until all eggs have been incorporated.
- Stir in chocolate chips.
- Pour filling into crust.
- Bake 40 minutes. Remove from oven and let stand 10 minutes.

Topping

2 cups sour cream
½ cup sugar
1 teaspoon almond extract

- Combine sour cream, almond extract and sugar.
- Spread topping evenly over top of baked filling.
- Return to oven and bake 10 minutes longer.
- Remove from oven and place immediately in refrigerator to prevent cracks in top.

Turtle Cheesecake

This cheesecake offers something for everyone—chocolate, caramel, and nuts.

Preparation: 45 minutes
Baking: 50 minutes plus cooling
Yield: 10-12 servings

1 cup graham cracker crumbs
1 cup chocolate wafer
  crumbs
6 tablespoons margarine,
  melted
1 (14 ounce) bag caramels
1 (5 ounce) can evaporated
  milk
1 cup chopped pecans,
  toasted
1 pound cream cheese,
  softened
½ cup sugar
1 teaspoon vanilla extract
2 eggs
pecan halves for garnish

- Preheat oven to 350°.
- In a small bowl, combine crumbs with margarine. Press onto bottom of 9-inch springform pan.
- Bake 10 minutes.
- In a 1½-quart saucepan, melt caramels and milk over low heat. Stir until smooth. Reserve ¼-½ cup sauce for topping. Pour remainder over crust.
- Sprinkle pecans over caramel layer.
- In a medium bowl, combine cream cheese, sugar and vanilla. Mix at medium speed until well blended.
- Add eggs, one at a time. Mix well after each addition. Pour over pecans.
- Place a 9x13-inch baking pan of water on center rack in oven. Increase oven temperature to 450°. When oven is ready, remove pan of water. Bake cheesecake for 10 minutes at 450°. Then reduce temperature to 250° and continue to bake for 30 minutes.
- At that time, turn oven off. Leave cheesecake in the closed oven for an additional 30 minutes. Do not open the oven door.
- At the end of that 30 minutes, crack oven door open with a hot pad and cool cheesecake another 30 minutes.
- Pour remaining caramel sauce over top. Garnish with pecan halves. When completely cool, refrigerate.

Chocolate Swirl Cheesecake

Chocolate lovers will especially love this!

Preparation: 45 minutes
Baking: 40-45 minutes
Yield: 10-12 servings

1 cup (6 ounces) semi-sweet chocolate chips
½ cup sugar
1¼ cups graham cracker crumbs
2 tablespoons sugar
¼ cup butter, melted
1 pound cream cheese, softened
¾ cup sugar
½ cup sour cream
1 teaspoon vanilla extract
4 eggs

- Preheat oven to 325°.
- Combine chocolate chips and ½ cup sugar in double boiler over hot, not boiling, water.
- Heat until chocolate is melted and mixture is smooth; set aside.
- Combine graham cracker crumbs, 2 tablespoons sugar and butter; mix well.
- Pat crumb mixture over bottom and 1 inch up sides of 9-inch springform pan.
- Beat cream cheese until light and creamy.
- Gradually add ¾ cup sugar, beating until smooth.
- Mix in sour cream and vanilla.
- Add eggs, one at a time, beating well after each addition.
- Divide batter in half.
- Stir melted chocolate mixture into ½ of batter.
- Leave remaining batter plain.
- Pour chocolate batter over crust in pan.
- Spoon plain batter over chocolate batter.
- Swirl batter with a knife.
- Bake 40-45 minutes.
- Cool at room temperature before removing rim from pan; refrigerate.

Chocolate Lemon Cheesecakes

Take two—they're small!

Preparation: 20 minutes
Baking: 12 minutes
Yield: 24 servings

Filling
½ cup cream cheese,
  softened
1 egg
2 tablespoons superfine
  sugar
1 tablespoon lemon juice

- Beat all ingredients until soft and smooth; set aside.

Chocolate Cake
¾ cup flour
½ cup superfine sugar
2 tablespoons unsweetened
  cocoa powder
½ teaspoon baking soda
½ teaspoon baking powder
pinch of salt
½ cup water
2 tablespoons vegetable oil
2 teaspoons lemon juice
1 teaspoon vanilla extract
2 eggs, separated

- Preheat oven to 350°.
- Sift flour with sugar, cocoa, baking soda, baking powder and salt.
- Add water, oil, lemon juice, vanilla and egg yolks. Beat mixture for 30 seconds.
- In small bowl, beat egg whites until stiff. Fold into chocolate mixture, ⅓ at a time.
- Fill greased miniature muffin pans half full with chocolate mixture.
- Place a teaspoon of filling in center of each cup.
- Bake 12 minutes or until set.

Chocolate Almond Cheesecake

Looks great, tastes great!

Preparation: 1 hour plus chilling
Baking: 35 minutes
Yield: 10-12 servings

Crust

**1½ cups chocolate wafer
    cookie crumbs**
**1 cup blanched almonds,
    lightly toasted, finely
    chopped**
⅓ cup sugar
**6 tablespoons butter,
    softened**

- Cookie crumbs and almonds may be chopped together in food processor.
- Combine all ingredients; mix well.
- Press into sides and bottom of buttered 9-inch springform pan.

Filling

**1½ pounds cream cheese,
    softened**
1 cup sugar
4 eggs
⅓ cup heavy cream
¼ cup amaretto liqueur
1 tablespoon vanilla extract

- Preheat oven to 375°.
- Cream together cream cheese and sugar.
- Add eggs, one at a time, beating well after each addition.
- Add heavy cream, amaretto liqueur and vanilla.
- Beat well until light.
- Pour over crust; bake 30 minutes.
- Place pan on wire rack for 5 minutes, while preparing topping.

Topping

2 cups sour cream
1 tablespoon sugar
1 tablespoon vanilla extract
slivered almonds

- Combine sour cream, sugar and vanilla; mix well.
- Spoon evenly over cheesecake.
- Bake an additional 5 minutes.
- Cool completely.
- Press slivered almonds around edge of cake to garnish.
- Refrigerate overnight.

Amaretto Cheesecake

Very subtle almond and amaretto flavor.

Preparation: 30 minutes
Baking: 1 hour
Yield: 8-12 servings

Crust
1½ cups crushed vanilla wafer crumbs
6 tablespoons margarine, melted
⅓ cup sugar
½ cup chopped almonds
½ cup chopped pecans
dash of salt

- Combine all ingredients and mix well.
- Press over bottom of 9-inch springform pan.

Filling
1½ pounds cream cheese, softened
1 (14 ounce) can sweetened condensed milk
3 eggs
1 teaspoon sugar
1 teaspoon almond extract
¼-⅓ cup amaretto liqueur

- Preheat oven to 350°.
- Blend cream cheese and condensed milk until smooth.
- Add eggs, sugar, almond extract and amaretto; blend until smooth.
- Pour over crust.
- Bake 1 hour.
- Remove from oven and allow to cool on wire rack 30 minutes.
- Refrigerate cheesecake at least 3 hours before serving.

Macadamia Nut Cheesecake

Not too sweet...just right!

Preparation: 40 minutes
Baking: 35-40 minutes
Yield: 12 servings

Crust
1½ cups graham cracker
crumbs
6 tablespoons margarine,
melted
¼ cup sugar
3 tablespoons unsweetened
cocoa powder

- Combine all ingredients and mix well.
- Press crumb mixture into bottom and partly up sides of greased 9-inch springform pan.
- Chill crust for 10 minutes in freezer until it is set.

Filling
12 ounces cream cheese,
softened
¾ cup sugar
1½ teaspoons vanilla extract
3 eggs
¾ cup chopped macadamia
nuts

- Preheat oven to 350°.
- Combine cream cheese, sugar and vanilla; mix until well blended.
- Add eggs one at a time, mixing well after each addition.
- Distribute nuts over crust. Place springform pan on baking sheet; pour in filling.
- Bake 35-40 minutes or until knife inserted in center comes out clean. Cool and refrigerate until serving.
- Garnish with whipped topping, whole macadamia nuts and chocolate curls.

Note: To make chocolate curls, use a vegetable parer
and room temperature chunks of semi-sweet dark chocolate.
Produce smooth shapes by drawing blade toward thumb
along chunk to form curl evenly.

Peanut Butter Ice Cream Cheesecake

A spectacular dessert that merits applause.

Preparation: 30-40 minutes plus several freezing steps
Yield: 12-16 servings

Crust
1 (8 ounce) package chocolate wafers, crushed
⅓ cup margarine, melted

- Mix together crushed wafers and melted margarine.
- Reserve ½ cup crumbs.
- Put remainder on bottom and ¾ of the way up sides of 10-inch springform pan.
- Freeze 30 minutes or until firm.

Filling
3 pints premium chocolate fudge ice cream, divided
2 eggs, separated
1 cup sugar, divided
1 cup whipping cream
8 ounces cream cheese, softened
1 teaspoon vanilla extract
¾ cup creamy peanut butter

- Soften and spread 2 pints of chocolate fudge ice cream on bottom and sides of prepared pan. Freeze 30 minutes or until firm.
- Beat egg whites until soft peaks form. Add ¼ cup sugar and beat until stiff. Set aside.
- Whip cream until stiff but not dry. Set aside.
- In a large bowl, beat together cream cheese, ¾ cup sugar, vanilla and peanut butter until smooth. Add egg yolks. Beat well.
- Fold in beaten egg whites and whipped cream.
- Pour into lined crust. Return to freezer to set, approximately one hour.
- Soften remaining 1 pint ice cream 10 minutes. Spread over whipped cream layer.
- Sprinkle with reserved crumbs.
- Return to freezer.
- Soften in refrigerator 10-20 minutes before serving.

Peaches and Cream Cheesecake

More like a cake than a cheesecake.

Preparation: 30 minutes
Baking: 30-35 minutes
Yield: 8-10 servings

Base
¾ **cup flour**
1 **teaspoon baking powder**
½ **teaspoon salt**
1 **small package**
   (approximately 3¾ ounces)
   dry vanilla pudding mix,
   not instant
3 **tablespoons butter or**
   margarine, softened
1 **egg**
½ **cup milk**

- Preheat oven to 350°.
- Combine all base ingredients in large bowl.
- Beat 2 minutes on medium speed.
- Pour into greased 9-inch springform pan.

Filling
1 **(16 ounce) can sliced**
   peaches, drained,
   reserving 3 tablespoons
   juice
8 **ounces cream cheese,**
   softened
½ **cup sugar**
1 **tablespoon sugar**
½ **teaspoon cinnamon**

- Place fruit over base batter.
- Combine cream cheese, sugar and reserved juice.
- Beat 2 minutes on medium speed.
- Spoon to within 1 inch of edge of batter.
- Mix sugar and cinnamon together.
- Sprinkle over cheese filling.
- Bake 30-35 minutes or until crust is golden brown. Filling will appear soft.
- Cool and refrigerate.

143

Praline Pecan Cheesecake

Rich and nutty.

Preparation: 1½ hours plus cooling and chilling
Baking: 1 hour
Yield: 12-14 servings

Crust
1 cup vanilla wafer crumbs
2 tablespoons sugar
¼ cup butter, softened

- Combine wafer crumbs, sugar and butter in small bowl. Mix thoroughly.
- Press into bottom of 9-inch springform pan. Chill.

Filling
1⅓ cups chopped pecans
3 tablespoons butter, softened
1½ pounds cream cheese, softened
1 cup firmly packed dark brown sugar
2 tablespoons flour
3 extra large eggs
1 teaspoon vanilla extract

- Preheat oven to 350°.
- Combine pecans and butter.
- Spread evenly on baking sheet.
- Toast until golden brown, watching carefully. Set aside to cool.
- Lower oven temperature to 325°.
- In large bowl, combine cream cheese, brown sugar and flour. Beat until light and fluffy.
- Add eggs, one at a time, blending well after each addition.
- Stir in vanilla.
- Reserving ¼ cup pecans for topping, add remaining pecans to filling mixture.
- Pour filling over crust and bake 1 hour.
- Turn off oven and allow cheesecake to cool in oven 30 minutes.
- Loosen cake from rim of pan.
- When cake has cooled to room temperature, remove rim. Prepare and add topping.

Topping

1½ teaspoons sugar
¼ cup firmly packed dark brown sugar
2 tablespoons heavy cream
1 tablespoon butter
½ teaspoon vanilla extract

- Combine sugars, cream and butter in small saucepan.
- Heat to boiling, stirring until sugars dissolve.
- Cook over low heat to just under soft ball stage or approximately 225° on candy thermometer.
- Immediately remove from heat and cool slightly.
- Add vanilla and stir until creamy.
- Sprinkle reserved pecans on top of cheesecake and drizzle praline mixture over pecans.
- Refrigerate 8 hours before serving.

Light Variation: Substitute Neufchâtel for cream cheese, margarine for butter and egg substitute for regular eggs.

Peach Cheesecake

Smooth, peachy and pleasant.

Preparation: 15 minutes plus overnight chilling
Baking: 1 hour
Yield: 16 servings

1½ pounds light cream cheese, softened
6 large eggs
1¾ cups sugar
2 (16 ounce) cans peaches, drained

- Preheat oven to 325°.
- Spread bottom and sides of 10-inch springform pan with butter.
- In a food processor, combine the cream cheese, eggs and sugar.
- Blend until smooth.
- Add peaches and process until smooth.
- Pour into prepared pan.
- Bake 1 hour.
- Turn off oven and let cheesecake cool in oven 20 minutes.
- Must refrigerate 24 hours before serving.

Mousse Cheesecake

*Adding a strawberry glaze
makes this an irresistible holiday
dessert!*

*Preparation: 45 minutes plus chilling
time*
Baking: 10-15 minutes for crust
Yield: 8-10 servings

Crust

**1½ cups graham cracker
    crumbs**
**¼ cup butter or margarine,
    melted**

- Preheat oven to 350°.
- Mix ingredients; press into 9-inch
  springform pan.
- Bake 10-15 minutes.

Filling

**2 envelopes unflavored
    gelatin**
**1 pound cream cheese,
    softened**
2 cups sugar
1 teaspoon vanilla extract
2 tablespoons lemon juice
4 eggs, separated
1 cup whipping cream

- Soften gelatin in ½ cup boiling water;
  cool.
- Beat cream cheese, sugar and vanilla.
- Beat in lemon juice and egg yolks.
- Stir in cooled gelatin.
- Beat egg whites until stiff.
- Beat whipping cream until soft peaks
  form.
- Fold egg whites into whipping cream; fold
  into cream cheese mixture.
- Pour into crust; chill until set.

*Variation: Filling may be served in stemmed glasses
garnished with fresh berries.*

Strawberry Glaze

*Terrific topping for cheesecake
or pound cake.*

Preparation: 15 minutes
Yield: ½ cup

**2 cups fresh strawberries,
    halved**
**1 tablespoon strawberry-
    flavored liqueur or water**
½ teaspoon cornstarch

- Place strawberries in a food processor or
  blender and process until smooth.
- Strain through a sieve to yield ½ cup
  purée.
- Combine purée, liqueur and cornstarch in
  a non-aluminum saucepan and bring to a
  boil.
- Cook 1 minute or until thickened; chill.
- Pour over top of cheesecake and spread
  evenly or serve on the side.

Frozen Mocha Mousse Cheesecake

Great coffee flavor.

Preparation: 20 minutes plus freezing
Yield: 8-10 servings

Crust

2 cups crushed chocolate wafers
½ cup butter, melted

- Mix crushed wafers and butter.
- Press into 9-inch pie plate and chill.

Filling

8 ounces cream cheese, softened
1 (14 ounce) can sweetened condensed milk
1 cup chocolate syrup
1 tablespoon instant coffee powder, mixed with 1 tablespoon hot water
1 teaspoon vanilla extract
8 ounces whipping cream, whipped

- Beat cream cheese.
- Add condensed milk, chocolate syrup, coffee and vanilla; mix very well.
- Fold in whipped cream.
- Pour over pie crust.
- Freeze until firm.
- Garnish with shaved chocolate if desired.

147

Mom's Cheesecake

No-fail dessert!

Preparation: 25 minutes
Baking: 35 minutes
Yield: Number of servings depends on
pan size

Crust
¾ **cup graham cracker**
  crumbs
2 **tablespoons margarine,**
  melted
2 **tablespoons sugar**

• Combine all ingredients and mix well.
• Press crumb mixture over bottom of 8-inch
  or 9-inch springform pan, 15x10x1-inch
  jelly roll pan or 8-inch square baking pan,
  any pan will do! Set aside.

Filling
1 **pound cream cheese,**
  softened
¾ **cup sugar**
5 **eggs**
1 **teaspoon vanilla extract**
1½ **teaspoons almond extract**

• Preheat oven to 350°.
• Combine cream cheese and sugar; mix
  well.
• Add eggs, vanilla and almond extract;
  blend.
• Spread over crust; bake 35 minutes.
• Remove from oven; cool 10 minutes.

Topping
1 **cup sour cream**
½ **teaspoon vanilla extract**
½ **teaspoon almond extract**
¼ **cup sugar**

• Increase oven temperature to 500°.
• Combine all topping ingredients; mix well.
• Spread over cake.
• Return to oven; bake 5 minutes.
• Chill before serving.

Pumpkin Cheesecake

Make 2 days ahead for best flavor.

Preparation: 30 minutes
Baking: 60 minutes
Yield: 10-12 servings

Crust
⅓ **cup butter, softened**
⅓ **cup sugar**
1 egg
1¼ cups flour

- Preheat oven to 400°.
- Cream butter and sugar.
- Add egg; blend well.
- Add flour and mix well.
- Press dough into bottom and 2 inches up sides of greased 9-inch springform pan.
- Bake 5 minutes.
- Remove from oven; reduce heat to 350°.

Filling
1 pound cream cheese, softened
¾ **cup sugar**
1 (16 ounce) can pumpkin
1½ teaspoons cinnamon
½ **teaspoon ginger**
¼ **teaspoon nutmeg**
2 eggs

- Beat cream cheese well; add sugar.
- Mix in pumpkin and spices.
- Add eggs, mixing well.
- Spread filling over crust.
- Bake 55 minutes. Loosen crust on all sides using a sharp knife. Cool before removing rim.
- Garnish with whipped cream flavored with rum extract.

Jay's Favorite Cheesecake

Very creamy cheesecake.

Preparation: 45 minutes
Baking: 40-50 minutes
Yield: 12 servings

2 cups graham cracker
  crumbs
⅓-½ cup margarine, melted
1 pound cream cheese,
  softened
1 cup sugar
2 tablespoons lemon juice
1 teaspoon vanilla extract
4 eggs

- Preheat oven to 350°.
- Mix cracker crumbs and margarine.
- Press into 9-inch springform pan.
- Beat cream cheese; blend in sugar, lemon juice and vanilla.
- Add eggs, one at a time, mixing well after each addition.
- Pour mixture over crust.
- Bake 25-30 minutes.

Topping
2 cups sour cream
¼ cup sugar
1 teaspoon vanilla extract

- Combine sour cream, sugar and vanilla extract.
- Spoon on top of hot cheesecake.
- Bake at additional 15-20 minutes.
- Cool and refrigerate.

Light Variation: Use light cream cheese, and egg and sour cream substitutes. Texture changes a little but flavor is still great.

Strawberry Cream Pie

Make this in the spring when strawberries are in season.

Preparation: 1 hour plus chilling
Yield: 6-8 servings

1 9-inch baked pie shell, cooled
3 tablespoons heavy cream
3 ounces cream cheese, softened
1½ quarts strawberries
1 cup sugar
2 tablespoons cornstarch
1 teaspoon lemon juice
1 cup whipping cream whipped and lightly sweetened

- Blend heavy cream and cream cheese until smooth.
- Spread evenly over cooled pie shell. Refrigerate.
- Reserve the most uniform berries, (about 1 quart) for top.
- Place remaining berries in a bowl with sugar and mash.
- Push through a fine sieve into small saucepan.
- Mix in cornstarch and lemon juice and cook over medium heat until thick and transparent. Cool.
- Place half of purée over cream cheese in pie shell.
- Arrange reserved berries (either whole or slice thickly) attractively on top, then pour remaining purée over all. Chill.
- Garnish with whipped cream just before serving.

Peach Pecan Pie

Orange you glad this one's a little different?

Preparation: 20-25 minutes
Baking: 55 minutes
Yield: 8 servings

1 cup sugar
3 tablespoons flour
2 tablespoons cornstarch
2 tablespoons orange juice
2 tablespoons butter
1 tablespoon grated orange peel
½ cup chopped pecans
2½ cups peeled and sliced peaches
1 9-inch unbaked pie shell

- Preheat oven to 450°.
- Mix sugar, flour and cornstarch in a saucepan.
- Add orange juice and butter and cook over low heat until thick.
- Remove from heat.
- Add orange peel, nuts and peaches; mix well.
- Pour mixture into pie shell.
- Bake at 450° for 10 minutes, then turn oven down to 325° and bake for 45 minutes.
- Serve with whipped cream.

Peach Pie

Attractively different.

Preparation: 15 minutes
Baking: 50 minutes
Yield: 8-10 servings

1 9-inch unbaked pie shell
3-4 peaches (enough to line pie pan when cut into halves) Choose your favorite freestone peach

- Peel peaches and cut in half, removing pit.
- Line pie shell with peach halves.

Filling
1 egg
1 teaspoon vanilla extract
1 cup sugar
½ cup butter, softened
2 tablespoons plus 1 teaspoon flour

- Preheat oven to 450°.
- Combine filling ingredients until smooth.
- Spread filling over and around peach halves.
- Bake at 450° for 10 minutes, reduce heat to 350°, bake additional 40 minutes.
- Cool on wire rack.

Raspberry Cream Cheese Pie

Good combination of flavors.

Preparation: 10 minutes plus chilling
Baking: 25 minutes
Yield: 6-8 servings

30 vanilla wafers, crushed
½ cup butter, melted
8 ounces cream cheese, softened
1 cup powdered sugar
1 teaspoon vanilla extract
1 cup non-dairy whipped topping
1 (10 ounce) box frozen raspberries, drained
3-4 chocolate toffee candy bars

- Preheat oven to 325°.
- Combine wafers and butter; pat into 9-inch pie plate.
- Bake 15 minutes. Turn off oven and leave crust in oven for 10 minutes; remove and cool.
- Mix cream cheese, powdered sugar, vanilla and whipped topping.
- Pour in raspberries.
- Mix and pour into crust.
- Crush candy bars in blender; sprinkle on top of pie.
- Chill 1 hour before serving.

Fresh Blueberry Cream Cheese Pie

The gingersnap crust gives this a special flavor.

Preparation: 90 minutes plus chilling
Baking: 10 minutes
Yield: 15-20 servings

Gingersnap Crust

2½ cups gingersnap cookie crumbs
⅓ cup butter, melted

- Preheat oven to 350°.
- Combine crumbs and butter; mix well.
- Press firmly over bottom of 9x13-inch baking pan.
- Bake 10 minutes; cool.

Cream Cheese Layer

8 ounces cream cheese, softened
1 (14 ounce) can sweetened condensed milk
⅓ cup lemon juice
1 teaspoon vanilla extract

- Beat cream cheese until light and fluffy.
- Stir in milk, lemon juice and vanilla; mix well.
- Pour over cooled crust; spread evenly.

Blueberry Layer

4½ cups fresh blueberries, divided
½ cup water
1 teaspoon lemon juice
1 cup sugar
3½ tablespoons cornstarch
12 ounces non-dairy whipped topping

- In a medium saucepan, combine 1½ cups blueberries, water, lemon juice, sugar and cornstarch.
- Cook, stirring constantly, until mixture is thickened. Cool slightly.
- Stir in remaining 3 cups blueberries.
- Pour over cream cheese layer.
- Cool 30 minutes.
- Top with whipped topping.
- Chill 2-3 hours before serving.

Indiana Lemon Angel Pie

Beautiful presentation and delicious too!

Preparation: 1 hour 15 minutes plus chilling
Baking: 1 hour
Yield: 8-10 servings

Meringue Shell
3 egg whites (reserving yolks for filling)
¼ teaspoon cream of tartar
1 cup sugar

- Preheat oven to 275°.
- Beat egg whites with cream of tartar until foamy white.
- Beat in sugar, one tablespoon at a time, until it forms stiff glossy peaks.
- Lightly butter a 9-inch pie plate.
- Spoon meringue over bottom and up sides to form a shell.
- Bake 1 hour; turn off oven and leave pie in oven until cool.

Lemon Filling
5 egg yolks
⅔ cup sugar
1 tablespoon grated lemon rind
⅓ cup lemon juice
1 cup heavy cream, whipped for garnish

- Beat egg yolks in top of double boiler until frothy.
- Beat in sugar slowly until mixture is thick and light colored.
- Stir in lemon rind and lemon juice.
- Cook, stirring constantly, in double boiler over hot, not boiling water, 10-15 minutes, until mixture is thick; cool.
- Spoon cooled mixture into meringue shell.
- Cover loosely; refrigerate overnight.
- Top with whipped cream and decorate with lemon slices.

Lemon Sponge Pie with Raspberry Sauce

This is a light pie. Great for holiday dinners.

Preparation: 20 minutes
Baking: 45 minutes
Yield: 8 servings

1 9-inch unbaked pie shell
1 tablespoon butter or margarine, softened
1 cup sugar
⅛ teaspoon salt
2 tablespoons flour
¼ cup fresh lemon juice (juice of 1 lemon)
1 teaspoon grated lemon peel
2 eggs, separated
1 cup milk

- Preheat oven to 425°.
- Bake pie shell for 10 minutes; cool.
- Reduce oven to 350°.
- Cream together butter and sugar.
- Add salt, flour, lemon juice and lemon peel.
- Beat egg yolks and add milk.
- Blend well with sugar mixture.
- Beat egg whites until stiff but not dry.
- Fold into filling mixture.
- Pour into partially baked pie shell.
- Bake 35 minutes or until golden brown.
- Serve with a dollop of whipped cream or Raspberry Sauce.

Raspberry Sauce

1 (10 ounce) package frozen raspberries or 1 quart fresh raspberries
sugar to taste

- Combine raspberries and sugar in saucepan.
- Heat to boiling.
- Reduce heat and simmer until the mixture is sauce consistency.
- Strain to remove seeds.

Key Lime Pie for a Crowd

*Looks and tastes like
springtime.*

*Preparation: 20 minutes plus chilling
Baking: 10 minutes
Yield: 15-20 servings*

Crust
1 cup flour
½ cup butter
½ cup chopped nuts

- Preheat oven to 350°.
- Place flour, butter and chopped nuts into workbowl of food processor.
- Pulse to combine.
- Press into a 9x13-inch baking dish.
- Bake 10 minutes.

Filling
⅓ cup water
**2 envelopes unflavored
  gelatin**
1 cup lime juice
1 tablespoon lime zest
**2 (14 ounce) cans sweetened
  condensed milk**
4 egg whites

- Soften gelatin in water for 1 minute.
- Heat gently just until gelatin is dissolved.
- Let cool 2-3 minutes.
- In large bowl, combine lime juice, lime zest and sweetened condensed milk.
- Add gelatin.
- Beat egg whites until stiff, but not dry.
- Fold egg whites into lime juice mixture.
- Pour into cooled crust.
- Refrigerate until ready to serve.
- Delicious served with whipped cream.

Sugarless Apple Tart

No sugar, but great taste.

*Preparation: 15 minutes
Baking: 10 minutes
Yield: 6-8 servings*

1 baked 9-inch pie shell
**5-7 apples, any type, peeled
  and chopped**
3 tablespoons butter
**½ cup sugarless raspberry
  spread**
½ cup chopped walnuts
whipped cream

- Sauté apples in butter until tender; place in cooled pie shell.
- Melt raspberry spread in microwave and pour over chopped apple mixture.
- Sprinkle with nuts.
- Top with whipped cream just before serving.

Orange Lemon Balm Chiffon Pie

*A low-calorie treat courtesy of
The Herb Cottage, Niles,
Michigan.*

*Preparation: 30 minutes plus chilling
Yield: 6-8 servings*

1 envelope unflavored gelatin
½ cup sugar
1 cup hot water
3 eggs, separated
1 teaspoon chopped chervil
**2 teaspoons chopped lemon
  balm**
¾ cup orange juice
3 tablespoons lemon juice
dash salt
**1 9-inch graham cracker
  crumb pie crust**

- Mix gelatin, sugar and salt in top of double boiler. Stir in water until gelatin is dissolved.
- Beat egg yolks.
- Add beaten egg yolks to gelatin mixture and cook until mixture coats spoon. Remove from heat.
- Add chervil, lemon balm and juices. Chill until mixture starts to set.
- Beat egg whites until stiff; fold into gelatin.
- Pour into crust. Chill 2 hours before serving.
- Garnish with whipped cream and lemon balm leaves.

Caramel Crunch Apple Pie

A Midwestern fall favorite.

*Preparation: 40 minutes
Baking: 50-60 minutes
Yield: 6-8 servings*

**4 cups peeled and sliced
  apples**
2 tablespoons water
28 vanilla caramels
¼ cup flour
½ cup sugar
½ teaspoon cinnamon
½ cup butter
**½ cup coarsely chopped
  walnuts**
1 9-inch unbaked pie shell

- Preheat oven to 375°.
- Heat caramels and water in top of double boiler, stirring until smooth.
- Layer ½ of apples and ½ of caramel sauce in pie shell; repeat.
- Combine flour, sugar and cinnamon.
- Cut in butter until mixture is crumbly.
- Add walnuts; sprinkle on top of pie.
- Bake 50-60 minutes until apples are tender.

Apple Walnut Pie

A dessert extravaganza from the Carriage House Restaurant, South Bend, Indiana.

Preparation: 30 minutes
Baking: 55 minutes
Yield: 8 servings

**4 cups canned apples,
  slightly drained**
6 tablespoons flour
1 cup sugar
1 teaspoon cinnamon
2 dashes nutmeg
½ cup raisins
1 9-inch unbaked pie shell

- Preheat oven to 375°.
- Mix ingredients together. Pour into pie shell.
- Bake 40 minutes. Remove pie from oven and reduce oven temperature to 350°.

Streusel Topping
**1 cup firmly packed brown
  sugar**
½ cup flour
½ cup butter, melted
2 teaspoons cinnamon
½ cup walnut pieces

- Mix together brown sugar, flour, butter and cinnamon.
- Spread topping over pie. Sprinkle with walnuts.
- Bake an additional 15 minutes. Cool slightly; glaze.

Glaze
1 cup powdered sugar
1 teaspoon vanilla extract
3 tablespoons butter, melted
cream to thin

- In small bowl, mix powdered sugar, vanilla and butter until smooth.
- Add enough cream to thin glaze to consistency of heavy cream.
- Pour over warm pie.

Dutch Apple Pie

This is the apple of my pie.

Preparation: *30 minutes*
Baking: *50 minutes*
Yield: *6-8 servings*

Crust
1½ cups flour
¼ teaspoon salt
½ cup shortening
3-4 tablespoons cold water

- Mix flour and salt in a bowl.
- Add shortening and work into the flour mixture with a pastry blender until it resembles fresh bread crumbs.
- Sprinkle on the water, one tablespoon at a time, stirring lightly with a fork after each addition. Use only enough water to hold dough together.
- Form dough into a ball.
- On lightly floured surface, roll dough from center to edge, until ⅛-inch thick and 2 inches larger than inverted 9-inch pie plate.
- Transfer dough to pie plate, trim and crimp the edges.

Filling
9 medium apples
3 tablespoons flour
1 cup sugar
¼ teaspoon ground cloves
1 cup sour cream
½ teaspoon cinnamon
1½ tablespoons sugar

- Preheat oven to 450°.
- Pare, core and slice apples into unbaked pie shell.
- Combine flour, 1 cup sugar and cloves; add sour cream and mix.
- Pour over apple slices.
- Sprinkle with cinnamon and 1½ tablespoons sugar.
- Bake at 450° for 10 minutes; reduce temperature to 350° and bake an additional 40 minutes, until apples are tender.

Katie's Apple Pie

Apple pies are comfort food.

Preparation: 45 minutes
Baking: 55 minutes
Yield: 8-10 servings

6 large cooking apples
3 tablespoons maraschino
   cherry juice
1-2 teaspoons cinnamon
1-1½ cups sugar
2 tablespoons cornstarch
½ cup butter
½ cup flour
½ cup sugar
½ cup chopped pecans
1 10-inch unbaked pie shell

- Preheat oven to 450°.
- Pare and slice apples.
- Toss apples with maraschino juice.
- Place ½ of the apples in unbaked pie shell.
- Combine cinnamon, sugar and cornstarch.
- Sprinkle ½ of this mixture over the apples.
- Place remaining apples in pie shell and sprinkle with remaining cinnamon-sugar mixture.
- Cut butter into flour and sugar until crumbly.
- Add nuts; sprinkle over apples.
- Bake on middle rack at 450° for 10 minutes. Reduce oven to 350° and bake for 45 minutes.

Pumpkin Lemon Cream Pie

The tartness of the lemon balances the pumpkin well.

Preparation: 20 minutes plus cooling
Baking: 1 hour 10 minutes
Yield: 8-10 servings

2 eggs, slightly beaten
1 (16 ounce) can pumpkin
⅔ cup sugar
1 teaspoon salt
1 teaspoon cinnamon
½ teaspoon ginger
1⅓ cups half-and-half
1 9-inch unbaked pie shell

- Preheat oven to 425°.
- Thoroughly mix all filling ingredients.
- Pour mixture into pie shell.
- Bake at 425° for 15 minutes, reduce heat to 350° and continue baking 45 minutes until knife comes out clean.
- Cool 20 minutes.

Sour Cream Topping
1 cup sour cream
2 tablespoons firmly packed
   brown sugar
1 tablespoon lemon juice
¼ cup chopped pecans

- Blend sour cream, brown sugar and lemon juice.
- Spread mixture evenly over pie.
- Sprinkle top with chopped pecans.
- Bake at 350° for 10 minutes.
- Serve hot or cold.

Pumpkin Paradise Pie

Pumpkin pie with a twist.

Preparation: 40 minutes
Baking: 65 minutes
Yield: 8 servings

8 ounces cream cheese, softened
¼ cup sugar
3 eggs, divided
1 9-inch unbaked pie shell
1¼ cups canned pumpkin
1 cup evaporated milk
¼ cup firmly packed brown sugar
½ teaspoon vanilla extract
¼ cup sugar
1 teaspoon cinnamon
¼ teaspoon nutmeg
½ cup chopped pecans
¼ cup butter
2 tablespoons flour
2 tablespoons firmly packed brown sugar

- Beat together cream cheese, ¼ cup sugar and 1 egg, slightly beaten, until smooth. Chill 30 minutes.
- Preheat oven to 350°.
- Spoon mixture into unbaked pie shell.
- Combine pumpkin, evaporated milk, 2 eggs, ¼ cup brown sugar, vanilla, ¼ cup sugar, cinnamon and nutmeg.
- Carefully pour pumpkin mixture over cream cheese in pie shell.
- Cover edges of pie shell with foil and bake 25 minutes.
- Remove foil; bake an additional 25 minutes.
- Combine pecans, butter, flour and 2 tablespoons brown sugar.
- Sprinkle pecan mixture over pie and bake an additional 10-15 minutes until knife comes out clean.
- Cool on wire rack.

Walnut Pie

Best made one day ahead, but kept unrefrigerated.

Preparation: 15 minutes
Baking: 45 minutes
Yield: 8-10 servings

3 eggs
½ cup firmly packed brown sugar
1 cup light corn syrup
¼ cup butter, melted
2 teaspoons cinnamon
¼ teaspoon salt
1 teaspoon vanilla extract
1 cup walnut pieces
1 9-inch unbaked pie shell

- Preheat oven to 375°.
- Beat eggs well. Blend in brown sugar, corn syrup, butter, cinnamon, salt and vanilla in that order.
- Stir in walnuts.
- Pour mixture into unbaked pie shell.
- Place on the lowest rack in oven; bake 45 minutes or until the filling jiggles only slightly when moved.
- Cool on wire rack at least 2 hours before serving.

Peanut Butter Pie

Very rich! Take a small piece.

Preparation: 20 minutes plus chilling
Yield: 10 servings

Chocolate Crust

1 cup (6 ounces) chocolate chips
½ cup butter or margarine
2½ cups crispy rice cereal

- Melt chocolate and butter in large pan over low heat or in microwave.
- Add cereal; stir well to coat.
- Pour into well-buttered 9-inch or 10-inch pie plate.

Filling

⅔ cup peanut butter
8 ounces cream cheese, softened
6 ounces non-dairy whipped topping
1 (14 ounce) can sweetened condensed milk
chocolate syrup

- Combine all ingredients except chocolate syrup.
- Beat together until smooth.
- Pour into pie shell.
- Swirl chocolate syrup in spiral pattern on top of pie. (A)
- Use a spoon to make decorative pattern in chocolate, drawing spoon from outside edge towards center of pie as shown. (B)
- Finished pie should look like this. (C)
- Chill until firm.
- Remove from refrigerator 15 minutes before serving.

A   **B**   **C**

Frozen Chocolate Pecan Pie

A rich and luscious way to end a meal.

Preparation: 40 minutes plus freezing
Yield: 6-8 servings

Frozen Pecan Crust
2 cups finely chopped pecans, toasted
5 tablespoons plus 1 teaspoon firmly packed brown sugar
5 tablespoons butter, chilled and cut into small pieces
2 teaspoons dark rum

- Blend all ingredients for crust until mixture holds together.
- Press into bottom and sides of 9-inch pie plate.
- Freeze at least 1 hour.

Filling
1 cup (6 ounces) semi-sweet chocolate chips
½ teaspoon instant coffee powder
4 eggs, room temperature
1 tablespoon dark rum
1 teaspoon vanilla extract
1½ cups whipping cream
3 tablespoons shaved semi-sweet chocolate

- Melt chocolate chips with coffee in top of double boiler over hot water.
- Remove from heat and whisk in egg, rum and vanilla.
- Whisk mixture until smooth.
- Let cool about 5 minutes.
- Whip 1 cup cream until stiff.
- Gently fold into chocolate mixture, blending completely.
- Pour into crust and freeze.
- One hour before serving remove from freezer and refrigerate.
- Whip remaining ½ cup cream.
- Dollop over pie.
- Sprinkle with chocolate shavings.

Variation: Almond or coffee flavored liqueur
may be substituted in equal measure for the rum.

Strawberry Chocolate Tart

Very elegant.

Preparation: 1 hour plus chilling time
Baking: 16-18 minutes
Yield: 8 servings

Sweet Butter Crust
1⅔ cups flour
¼ cup sugar
½ teaspoon salt
10 tablespoons unsalted
  butter, chilled
2 egg yolks
1 teaspoon vanilla extract
2 teaspoons cold water

- Combine flour, sugar and salt in workbowl of food processor. Pulse to combine.
- Cut chilled butter into pieces; add to flour mixture.
- Pulse butter and dry ingredients until the mixture resembles coarse meal.
- Stir egg yolks, vanilla and cold water together.
- Add to flour mixture. Process until mixture forms a ball.
- Continue to process for 20-30 seconds to knead dough.
- Place dough onto wax paper. Form into a ball. Wrap in wax paper and chill for 2-3 hours.
- Preheat oven to 425°.
- Roll out dough between two sheets of wax paper into a round large enough to fit pan. Work quickly, as the dough can become sticky.
- Place dough in an 8-inch or 9-inch tart pan with removable bottom, fitting dough loosely into pan and pressing to fit sides.
- Trim edges ¾-inch outside top of pan and fold over to inside, pressing into place.
- Line dough in tart pan with aluminum foil and weight with rice or beans. Bake 8 minutes.
- Remove foil and beans. Prick bottom of dough in several places.
- Return to oven for 8-10 minutes longer, or until edges are light brown.

Filling

1 cup (6 ounces) milk
    chocolate or semi-sweet
    chocolate pieces
2 tablespoons unsalted
    butter, melted
4 tablespoons kirsch or
    cherry-flavored brandy,
    divided
¼ cup powdered sugar, sifted
1 tablespoon water
1 quart medium-sized
    strawberries, washed,
    hulled and dried
3 tablespoons red currant
    jelly

- In microwave safe bowl, melt chocolate on high for 1 minute. Stir until smooth.
- Add melted butter and 3 tablespoons kirsch, whisking until smooth.
- Add powdered sugar and water, continuing to whisk until smooth.
- While still warm, pour into tart shell.
- Place berries, tips up, over the warm chocolate filling in a circular pattern, working from the outside in. Cover entire surface.
- Warm currant jelly and remaining table-spoon kirsch over medium heat until melted and smooth.
- Brush over berries.
- Refrigerate for at least 2 hours.
- Remove from refrigerator 45 minutes before serving.

Kahlúa Pie

A grown-up dessert!

Preparation: 30 minutes plus freezing
Baking: 10 minutes
Yield: 8 servings

Chocolate Wafer Crust

1¼ cups chocolate wafer
    crumbs
6 tablespoons butter, melted
½ cup finely chopped nuts
1 tablespoon sugar

- Preheat oven to 350°.
- Combine ingredients and mix well.
- Pat into greased 9-inch pie plate.
- Bake 10 minutes. Cool.

Filling

2 cups whipping cream
1 teaspoon vanilla extract
⅓ cup Kahlúa liqueur
4 chocolate toffee candy
    bars, crushed
1 quart coffee ice cream,
    softened
whipped cream and grated
    chocolate for garnish

- Whip cream until stiff.
- Add vanilla and liqueur to whipped cream.
- Gently fold in crushed candy.
- Gently combine whipped cream mixture and softened ice cream.
- Spoon into pie shell; freeze.
- Remove from freezer 15 minutes before serving and garnish with whipped cream and grated chocolate.

Chocolate Mousse Pie

Like eating a floating cloud!

Preparation: 1 hour plus chilling
Yield: 12-16 servings

Chocolate Wafer Crust
3 cups chocolate wafer crumbs
½ cup butter, melted

- Combine crumbs and butter.
- Press on bottom and completely up the sides of 10-inch springform pan.
- Refrigerate 30 minutes or chill in freezer.

Filling
1 pound semi-sweet chocolate
2 eggs
4 egg yolks
4 cups whipping cream, divided
6 tablespoons powdered sugar
4 egg whites, room temperature
3 tablespoons sugar

- Melt chocolate in top of double boiler over simmering water.
- Let cool to lukewarm.
- Add whole eggs and mix well.
- Add egg yolks and mix until thoroughly blended.
- Whip 2 cups whipping cream with powdered sugar until soft peaks form.
- Beat egg whites until stiff but not dry.
- Stir a small amount of the cream and egg whites into the chocolate mixture to lighten.
- Fold in remaining cream and egg whites.
- Turn into crust and chill at least 6 hours or preferably overnight.
- Whip remaining 2 cups whipping cream with sugar, until quite stiff.
- Loosen crust on all sides using a sharp knife; remove springform sides.
- Spread whipping cream over top of mousse.
- Garnish with shaved chocolate.

Peppermint Pie

Delicious, refreshing dessert.

Preparation: 45 minutes plus freezing
Yield: 8 servings

2 cups (12 ounces) semi-
  sweet chocolate chips
6 tablespoons butter or
  margarine
2 cups oven-toasted rice
  cereal
½ cup chopped walnuts
½ cup milk
1 quart peppermint ice
  cream, slightly softened
crushed peppermint candy

- In a medium saucepan, melt 1 cup chocolate chips with 2 tablespoons butter. Remove from heat.
- Stir in cereal and walnuts.
- Spread over bottom and sides of a well-buttered 9-inch pie plate. Chill until firm.
- In a small saucepan, combine remaining chocolate pieces and butter with milk.
- Heat slowly, stirring constantly, until chocolate melts and sauce is smooth. Cool and set aside.
- Spoon ice cream into pie shell and freeze until serving time.
- At serving time, drizzle several spoonfuls of chocolate over pie. Sprinkle with crushed peppermint.
- Cut pie into wedges and serve with remaining chocolate.

Variation: Substitute mint chocolate chip ice cream
for the peppermint and omit crushed candies.

Brown Sugar Oatmeal Pie

Tastes like a cross between
oatmeal cookies and pecan pie.

Preparation: 15 minutes
Baking: 35-45 minutes
Yield: 8-10 servings

⅔ cup sugar
⅔ cup firmly packed brown
  sugar
3 eggs
⅔ cup uncooked oatmeal
⅔ cup coconut
3 tablespoons butter, melted
2 teaspoons vanilla extract
½ cup chopped pecans
1 9-inch unbaked pie shell

- Preheat oven to 350°.
- In large bowl, combine all filling ingredients.
- Pour into the unbaked pie shell.
- Bake 35-45 minutes or until top is well browned and center is set.
- If filling browns quickly, lower oven temperature to 325°.
- Let cool on wire rack.
- Serve warm with ice cream or whipped cream.

Cheshire Pie

A good old-fashioned coconut pie.

Preparation: 10 minutes
Baking: 50 minutes
Yield: 8-12 servings

½ cup margarine or butter, softened
1½ cups sugar
3 eggs
1 teaspoon cornmeal
1 teaspoon vinegar
1 tablespoon vanilla extract
1 teaspoon cornstarch
1½ cups flaked coconut
1 9-inch unbaked pie shell

- Preheat oven to 325°.
- Cream margarine and sugar together.
- Add eggs one at a time, mixing well after each addition.
- Add remaining filling ingredients, putting coconut in last.
- Pour filling into crust.
- Bake 50 minutes.

Rolled Pie Crust

Just like Mom's!

Preparation: 20 minutes
Baking: 10-12 minutes
Yield: one 9-inch or 10-inch pie crust

1½ cups flour
¼ teaspoon salt
½ cup shortening
3-4 tablespoons cold water

- Preheat oven to 450°.
- Stir flour and salt together in mixing bowl.
- With pastry blender, work in shortening until the mixture resembles fresh bread crumbs.
- Sprinkle on the water, 1 tablespoon at a time, stirring lightly with a fork after each addition. The dough should hold together, but not be sticky.
- Form dough into a flattened ball.
- Roll out on a lightly floured surface until ⅛-inch thick and 2 inches larger than pie plate.
- Transfer dough to pie plate.
- Trim dough and crimp edges as desired.
- Prick crust with a fork.
- If baking before filling, bake 10-12 minutes or until golden brown.

Vanilla Pecan Pie Crust

Tastes as good as it sounds.

Preparation: 10 minutes
Baking: 10 minutes
Yield: 1 10-inch pie crust

1½ **cups vanilla wafer crumbs**
½ **cup butter, melted**
1 **tablespoon sugar**
½ **cup crushed pecans**

- Preheat oven to 400°.
- Mix all ingredients together.
- Press into 10-inch pie plate.
- Bake 10 minutes at 400°.
- Cool completely.

No-Roll Pie Crust

Finally! A pie crust that doesn't have to be rolled out.

Preparation: 10 minutes
Baking: 10-12 minutes
Yield: 1 (9-inch) pie crust

1½ **cups flour**
½ **cup oil**
½ **teaspoon salt**
1 **tablespoon sugar**
2 **tablespoons milk**

- Preheat oven to 400°.
- Mix all ingredients together in pie plate.
- Press into bottom and sides of pie plate.
- Bake 10-12 minutes or until golden brown.

Sour Cream Apple Squares

The entire family will love this.

Preparation: 25 minutes
Baking: 25-35 minutes
Yield: 12-15 servings

2 cups flour
2 cups firmly packed brown sugar
½ cup butter, softened
1 cup chopped nuts
1-2 teaspoons cinnamon
1 teaspoon baking soda
½ teaspoon salt
1 cup sour cream
1 teaspoon vanilla extract
1 egg
2 cups peeled, finely chopped apples (about 2 medium apples)

- Preheat oven to 350°.
- Combine in large bowl, flour, brown sugar and butter.
- Blend on low speed until crumbly.
- Stir in nuts.
- Press 3¾ cups of the mixture into ungreased 9x13-inch baking pan.
- Mix cinnamon, baking soda, salt, sour cream, vanilla and egg. Blend well and add to remaining nut mixture.
- Stir in apples.
- Spoon evenly over the base mixture.
- Bake 25-35 minutes; do not overbake.
- Cut into squares; serve with whipped cream or vanilla ice cream.

Blueberries and Cheese Squares

Made with the blueberry lover in mind.

Preparation: 20 minutes
Yield: 10-12 servings

10 whole graham crackers, crushed
½ cup butter or margarine, melted
8 ounces cream cheese, softened
¼ cup milk
4 tablespoons powdered sugar, divided
1 (21 ounce) can blueberry pie filling
1 cup whipping cream

- Combine graham cracker crumbs and butter.
- Reserve ½ crumb mixture for top; press remainder into bottom of 7x11-inch pan. Chill briefly.
- Blend cream cheese, milk and 2 table-spoons powdered sugar.
- Spread over crumb layer.
- Spread pie filling over cheese layer and chill while preparing whipped cream.
- Using a chilled bowl and beaters, beat the whipping cream with 2 tablespoons powdered sugar until stiff; spread over berries.
- Sprinkle with reserved crumb mixture and refrigerate until ready to serve.

Easy Peach-Raspberry Cobbler

"Looks beautiful—tastes wonderful!"

Preparation: 15 minutes
Baking: 20-25 minutes
Yield: 6-8 servings

Filling
3 cups peeled, sliced peaches
1 cup fresh or frozen dry-
pack raspberries
⅓-½ cup sugar
1 tablespoon butter

- Preheat oven to 400°.
- Combine peaches, raspberries and sugar; toss to mix.
- Pour fruit into 9-inch or 10-inch glass pie plate.
- Dot with butter.

Dough
1 cup flour
1 tablespoon sugar
1½ teaspoons baking powder
½ teaspoon salt
¼ teaspoon cinnamon
2 tablespoons cold butter or
margarine
scant ½ cup half-and-half
powdered sugar for garnish

- Measure dry ingredients into food processor.
- Cut butter into several pieces; add to food processor.
- Pulse until butter pieces are size of small peas.
- Slowly pour half-and-half in through the feed tube with the motor running.
- Process only until dough begins to hold together.
- On floured surface, roll out dough to a circle slightly smaller than size of pie plate.
- Crimp or trim edges as desired.
- Place dough on top of fruit; cut slashes for steam to escape.
- Bake 20-25 minutes or until golden brown.
- Sift powdered sugar over top.
- Serve warm with cream or half-and-half.

Fruit Belt Cobbler

An old-fashioned treat.

Preparation: 10 minutes
Baking: 45 minutes

¼ cup butter or margarine
½ cup sugar
1 cup flour
¼ teaspoon salt
2 teaspoons baking powder
½ cup milk
3-4 cups fresh, frozen or
   canned fruit—cherries,
   blueberries, peaches, etc.
¼-½ cup sugar
¼ teaspoon cinnamon
1½ cups "compatible" fruit
   juice, water or combination
   of juice and water

- Preheat oven to 375°.
- Cream butter and sugar until fluffy.
- Mix flour, salt and baking powder.
- Add to butter mixture alternately with milk.
- Pour into greased shallow 2-quart casserole; spread evenly.
- Wash fresh fruit or drain frozen or canned fruits, reserving juice.
- Spoon fruit over batter.
- Mix sugar and cinnamon; sprinkle evenly over fruit. Sugar may be eliminated if using canned fruit.
- Pour fruit juice over top.
- Bake 45 minutes or until golden brown.
- Serve warm with cream, half-and-half or ice cream.

Gourmet Strawberries

Simple and elegant.

Preparation: 20 minutes
Yield: 8-10 servings

8 ounces cream cheese,
   softened
6 tablespoons sugar
1½ cups sour cream
1 teaspoon vanilla extract
1 quart strawberries, cleaned
   and halved

- In a medium bowl, beat cream cheese, sugar, sour cream, and vanilla until smooth.
- Divide strawberries evenly among sherbet glasses or small bowls, reserving enough halves for garnish.
- Top strawberries with a dollop of cream cheese mixture.
- Top each serving with a strawberry half for garnish.

Layered Fruit Dessert

Great light summer dessert.

Preparation: 30 minutes
Yield: 24 (½-cup) servings

Topping

3 ounces cream cheese,
  softened
8 ounces strawberry yogurt
1 tablespoon sugar
2 teaspoons lemon juice
2 cups non-dairy whipped
  topping, thawed
¼ teaspoon almond extract

- Combine cream cheese, yogurt, sugar and lemon juice; beat until smooth.
- Add whipped topping and almond extract.
- Beat until smooth and thick; refrigerate.

Fruit

2 cups fresh blueberries
3 ripe peaches, peeled and
  sliced
2 cups fresh strawberries,
  washed, drained and
  halved
2 cups seedless green grapes
1 (20 ounce) can mandarin
  oranges, well-drained
2 tablespoons sliced
  almonds, toasted

- Layer blueberries, peaches and strawberries in parfait glasses or in large glass bowl.
- Spoon ½ of topping mixture on top of fruit to cover.
- Layer grapes and oranges over topping mixture.
- Spoon remainder of topping over fruit.
- Sprinkle with almonds.

Honeyed Green Grapes

Refreshing after a heavy meal.

Preparation: 10 minutes plus chilling
Yield: 8 servings

1 pound seedless grapes
1 teaspoon lemon juice
¼ cup honey
2 tablespoons brandy
½ cup sour cream

- Wash and drain grapes; remove stems.
- Mix lemon juice, honey and brandy to make a sauce.
- Pour sauce over grapes to cover; chill.
- Serve in sherbet or champagne glasses with a dollop of sour cream.

English Trifle

Layer in a trifle bowl for a pretty centerpiece.

Preparation: 1 hour
Yield: 8 servings

¼ cup rum or bourbon
1 cup sliced almonds
sponge cake or pound cake, cubed
3 small (approximately 3¾ ounce) packages instant French vanilla pudding mix
6 cups half-and-half
1 cup each raspberries, blueberries and strawberries
1 cup whipping cream, whipped
nutmeg

- Combine rum and almonds.
- Pour over cubed cake and marinate.
- Prepare pudding as directed on package using half-and-half instead of milk.
- Layer in trifle bowl making several layers; marinated cake, fruit mixture and pudding.
- Top with whipped cream; sprinkle with nutmeg.

Amaretti Dessert

Five-star recipe.

Preparation: 20 minutes plus freezing
Yield: 10 servings

2 cups heavy cream
1 cup sugar
½ cup finely crushed Amaretti di Saronna cookies
3 ounces semi-sweet chocolate, grated
6 egg whites
½ cup Amaretti di Saronna cookies, whole
Chocolate Whipped Cream for garnish

- Beat heavy cream until thick.
- Gradually add sugar and cookie crumbs.
- Beat until stiff peaks form.
- Fold in chocolate.
- In separate bowl, beat egg whites until stiff.
- Gently fold in cream mixture.
- Line 9x5-inch loaf pan with wax paper.
- Arrange whole cookies in bottom of pan. Spoon cream mixture into pan.
- Cover with plastic wrap. Freeze overnight until firm.
- Garnish with Chocolate Whipped Cream.

Chocolate Whipped Cream

1 cup whipping cream
½ cup chocolate syrup
2 tablespoons powdered sugar
1 teaspoon vanilla extract

- In a small mixing bowl, combine all ingredients.
- Beat until soft peaks form.

Chocolate Truffle Loaf with Raspberry Sauce

*From Service America
Corporation, in-house caterer at
Century Center, South Bend.*

*Preparation: 45 minutes plus chilling
Yield: 12 servings*

2 cups heavy cream, divided
3 egg yolks, slightly beaten
**1 pound semi-sweet
    chocolate**
**½ cup light or dark corn
    syrup**
½ cup margarine or butter
¼ cup powdered sugar
1 teaspoon vanilla extract

- Line 8½x4½x2½-inch loaf pan with plastic wrap.
- Mix ½ cup cream with egg yolks.
- In a medium saucepan, combine chocolate, corn syrup and margarine.
- Cook over medium heat, stirring occasionally, until melted.
- Add egg mixture.
- Stirring constantly, cook 3 minutes. Cool to room temperature.
- Beat remaining 1½ cups cream, sugar and vanilla until soft peaks form.
- Fold into chocolate mixture until no streaks remain.
- Pour into prepared pan.
- Refrigerate overnight or chill in freezer 3 hours. Serve with sauce.

Raspberry Sauce
**1 (10 ounce) package frozen
    raspberries, thawed**
⅓ cup light corn syrup

- Purée raspberries in blender; strain.
- Stir in corn syrup until well blended.

GiGi's Tirami Sŭ

Courtesy of Marigold Market, Granger, Indiana.

Preparation: 15 minutes
Yield: 6-8 servings

5 eggs, separated
6 tablespoons sugar
¾ pound mascarpone cheese
2 (4½ ounce) boxes lady
  fingers or savoiardi
1½ cups espresso coffee
½ cup chunk chocolate
  (optional)
¼ cup grated chocolate

- Beat sugar with egg yolks until mixture is creamy and pale.
- Beat egg whites until soft peaks form.
- Add mascarpone to egg yolk mixture and fold in whites.
- Dip lady fingers, a few at a time, into espresso coffee and place in single layer in bottom of decorative glass serving dish.
- Spread a layer of mascarpone mixture over lady fingers; repeat layers until all ingredients are used, ending with a layer of mascarpone.
- If desired, add chocolate chunks to each layer.
- Sprinkle top with grated chocolate.
- Chill until serving time.

Raspberry Rhapsody

You will want a second slice when no one is looking!

Preparation: 40 minutes plus freezing
Yield: 10-12 servings

2 cups whipping cream
1½ cups powdered sugar,
  sifted
2 tablespoons cream sherry
½ cup chopped pecans
1 quart raspberry sherbet

- Whip whipping cream.
- Add powdered sugar, sherry and pecans.
- Pour ½ of this mixture into 9-inch springform pan.
- Spread raspberry sherbet over this mixture.
- Add remaining whipped cream mixture and spread.
- Freeze overnight.

Raspberry Sauce
2 (10 ounce) packages frozen
  raspberries
½ cup sugar
¼ cup water
4 teaspoons lemon juice
6 tablespoons cream sherry

- Mix all ingredients, except sherry, in a saucepan.
- Boil gently 5 minutes.
- Add sherry and simmer 5 minutes longer. Cool.
- To serve, pour sauce over individual servings of frozen mixture.

Frozen Caramel Crunch

Can be kept frozen for several days.

Preparation: 15 minutes plus freezing
Baking: 15 minutes
Yield: 15 servings

1 cup butter, melted
½ cup firmly packed brown
  sugar
½ cup oatmeal
2 cups flour
½ cup chopped pecans
½ gallon vanilla ice cream,
  softened
2 (12 ounce) bottles caramel
  topping

- Preheat oven to 350°.
- Combine butter, brown sugar, oatmeal, flour, and pecans until crumbly.
- Spread mixture on jelly roll pan.
- Bake for 15 minutes or until lightly browned.
- Put ½ of crumb mixture into greased 9x13-inch baking pan. Do not press down.
- Spread ½ of softened ice cream on top of crumb mixture.
- Drizzle 1 bottle caramel topping over ice cream.
- Sprinkle remaining crumbs over caramel. Spread with ice cream and then drizzle with remaining caramel.
- Freeze 6 hours or overnight.

Chocolate Marshmallow Ice Cream

Great ice cream made without an ice cream freezer.

Preparation: 40 minutes plus freezing
Yield: 8-10 servings

2 ounces unsweetened
  chocolate
½ cup evaporated milk
  diluted with ½ cup water
16 large marshmallows
¼ cup sugar
⅛ teaspoon salt
1 cup evaporated milk,
  chilled for whipping
1 tablespoon lemon juice
½ cup chopped pecans
  (optional)

- Heat chocolate and diluted evaporated milk in double boiler until chocolate is melted.
- Add marshmallows, sugar and salt; heat slowly until marshmallows are melted. Chill.
- Whip chilled evaporated milk until stiff.
- Gently fold in lemon juice and chilled chocolate mixture.
- Add pecans if desired.
- Place in square pan or individual serving dishes and freeze at least 3 hours before serving.

Raspberry Ice Cream

Wonderful flavor—lovely pink color.

2 cups sugar
¼ cup cornstarch
¼ teaspoon salt
2 quarts half-and-half,
  divided
4 eggs, beaten
2 quarts fresh raspberries or
  2 (16 ounce) bags frozen
  dry-pack raspberries
1 tablespoon vanilla extract
½ cup framboise liqueur
ice cream freezer

Preparation: 20 minutes plus freezing
Yield: 1 gallon

- Combine sugar, cornstarch, and salt in 3-quart saucepan.
- Add 1 quart half-and-half. Cook over medium heat, stirring constantly, until thickened.
- Whisk 1 cup of hot half-and-half mixture into beaten eggs, then add warmed egg mixture to remaining half-and-half mixture. Stir vigorously while doing this, so eggs do not curdle. Cook 2-3 minutes more.
- Remove from heat and add raspberries, vanilla, and framboise.
- Pour into freezer can. Add remaining half-and-half. Stir to mix.
- Freeze according to manufacturer's directions.
- Transfer to freezer to help firm up ice cream.

Cheesecake Ice Cream

Very refreshing, even on a cold winter night.

2 egg yolks
1 cup sugar, divided
1 cup half-and-half
1 pound cream cheese, softened
1 teaspoon grated lemon rind
1 teaspoon grated orange rind
1 tablespoon lemon juice
½ teaspoon vanilla extract
2 cups plain yogurt
ice cream freezer

Preparation: 2½ hours, including freezing
Yield: 6-8 servings

- In a heavy saucepan, beat egg yolks with ½ cup sugar.
- Add half-and-half. Beat well.
- Cook over low heat, stirring constantly, just until thick enough to coat back of spoon. Do not boil.
- Remove from heat. Chill thoroughly.
- In a large bowl, beat cream cheese until light.
- Add ½ cup sugar, lemon and orange rinds, lemon juice and vanilla. Beat until smooth.
- Add yogurt and chilled egg mixture. Mix thoroughly.
- Freeze in an ice cream freezer according to manufacturer's directions.
- Serve with fresh fruit.

Frozen Praline Dessert

This may also be served in individual sherbet glasses.

1½ cups chopped pecans
½ cup firmly packed brown sugar
3 tablespoons butter, melted
1 (7 ounce) jar marshmallow creme
½ cup maple syrup
2 cups whipping cream

Preparation: 20 minutes plus freezing
Baking: 10 minutes
Yield: 15 servings

- Preheat oven to 350°.
- Combine pecans, brown sugar, and butter.
- Spread mixture on jelly roll pan.
- Bake 10 minutes. Cool and crumble.
- Mix marshmallow creme and maple syrup.
- In a separate bowl, whip the cream until stiff but not dry.
- Fold whipping cream into marshmallow creme mixture.
- Fold ½ of crumbled pecan mixture into marshmallow creme mixture.
- Spread into 9x13-inch baking pan or glass dish.
- Sprinkle remaining pecan mixture over top.
- Freeze overnight.

Frozen Strawberry Crumble

Perfect after a "heavy" meal.

Preparation: 30 minutes plus chilling
Baking: 10-15 minutes
Yield: 15-20 servings

1½ cups flour
½ cup firmly packed brown sugar
½ cup finely chopped nuts
½ cup margarine
3 egg whites
1 cup sugar (less if using sweetened frozen berries)
1 (16 ounce) package frozen strawberries, coarsely chopped in food processor
2 teaspoons lemon juice
12 ounces non-dairy whipped topping

- Preheat oven to 350°.
- Mix together flour, brown sugar, nuts and margarine.
- Place in 9x13-inch baking pan and bake 10-15 minutes, stirring every 5 minutes until evenly browned.
- Remove and reserve ⅓ of crumb mixture for topping.
- Press remaining crumb mixture into bottom of baking pan to form crust.
- Combine egg whites, sugar, berries, and lemon juice in very large mixing bowl. Beat at high speed until very stiff, about 10 minutes. This will increase in volume 3 or 4 times.
- Gently fold in whipped topping.
- Pour into crumb-lined pan. Top with reserved crumbs.
- Chill or freeze several hours or overnight.

Pink Peppermint Soufflé

As light and fluffy as a peppermint cloud.

Preparation: 45 minutes plus chilling
Yield: 8 servings

1 envelope unflavored gelatin
½ cup cold water
¾ cup crushed peppermint
  candy, divided
¼ cup white crème de
  menthe
3 egg whites
dash of salt
¼ cup sugar
1½ cups whipping cream

- Make a collar on a 4-cup soufflé dish with a double band of aluminum foil to extend 2 inches above the top of the dish.
- Grease band with vegetable oil.
- Fasten the foil together with paper clips or straight pins.
- In small saucepan, sprinkle gelatin over cold water to soften.
- Stir in ½ cup candy.
- Stir constantly over low heat, until gelatin and candy are dissolved, approximately 5 minutes.
- Remove from heat, let stand at room temperature until pan is cool to touch, but not longer than 30 minutes.
- Stir in crème de menthe.
- In small mixing bowl, beat egg whites and salt until foamy.
- Gradually beat in sugar.
- Beat until stiff and glossy.
- Place meringue mixture in large mixing bowl and fold in gelatin mixture. Add 3 tablespoons candy.
- Beat whipping cream until stiff; fold into meringue mixture.
- Pour into soufflé dish.
- Refrigerate 6 hours or overnight.
- Garnish with remaining candy before serving.

Lemon Soufflé with Raspberry Sauce

A lemon lover's delight.

Preparation: 1-1½ hours
Yield: 8-10 servings

Soufflé

2 envelopes unflavored
  gelatin
2 tablespoons cold water
8 eggs, separated
2 cups sugar, divided
1 cup lemon juice (juice of 3
  whole lemons)
1½ teaspoons grated lemon
  rind
3 cups whipping cream

- Sprinkle gelatin over water; let stand.
- Beat egg yolks with 1 cup sugar until light and fluffy.
- Combine egg yolk mixture and lemon juice in top of double boiler. Cook, stirring constantly, until thickened and custard-like.
- Add gelatin and lemon rind, stirring constantly.
- Turn into large bowl and cool slightly.
- Beat egg whites until stiff but not dry.
- Add 1 cup sugar; beat until stiff peaks form.
- Fold into custard.
- Whip the cream; fold into custard.
- To prepare collar for soufflé dish, fold a long strip of aluminum foil lengthwise and oil 1 side. Use paper clips or straight pins to fasten it around edges of a 1½-quart soufflé dish, oiled side in. Collar should stand 3 inches above top of dish.
- Fill prepared soufflé dish with custard; refrigerate.
- This may be prepared up to 10 hours before serving.

Raspberry Sauce

1 (10 ounce) package frozen
  raspberries or 1 pint fresh
  raspberries
sugar to taste
2-3 tablespoons orange-
  flavored liqueur

- Combine raspberries and sugar in small saucepan; bring to a boil.
- Reduce heat and simmer until mixture is sauce consistency.
- Remove from heat and strain.
- Add liqueur; blend well.
- Serve over soufflé.

Mini Chocolate Soufflés

Make ahead and bake during dinner. Never fails to rise!

Preparation: 20 minutes
Baking: 15 minutes
Yield: 8 servings

**8 ounces semi-sweet
  chocolate**
1 tablespoon butter
1 tablespoon flour
½ cup milk
3 egg yolks
1 teaspoon vanilla extract
**1-2 tablespoons almond-
  flavored liqueur**
4 egg whites
⅛ teaspoon cream of tartar
¼ cup sugar
**2-3 tablespoons powdered
  sugar, for dusting**
whipped cream

- Preheat oven to 375°.
- Lightly butter eight 6-ounce ramekins or custard cups.
- Dust with granulated sugar; place on baking sheet.
- Melt chocolate in top of double boiler, stirring occasionally, until smooth; remove from heat.
- Melt butter in a saucepan.
- Stir in flour; cook until thickened but not browned, about 1-2 minutes.
- Add milk; whisk until smooth and thick, about 3 minutes.
- Remove from heat, add melted chocolate and whisk until smooth.
- Whisk in the egg yolks, vanilla and liqueur; set aside.
- Beat the egg whites and cream of tartar at medium speed until soft peaks form, about 1 minute.
- Gradually sprinkle sugar on top; beat on high speed until stiff but not dry.
- Fold ¼ of the egg whites into the chocolate mixture to lighten; fold in remaining egg whites.
- Spoon mixture into prepared ramekins, filling ¾ full.
- Can be prepared to this point up to 1 day ahead. Cover and refrigerate.
- Bake 15 minutes until puffed and slightly cracked.
- Dust with powdered sugar.
- Serve immediately with whipped cream.

*Variation: Substitute orange or other
favorite flavored liqueur for almond-flavored liqueur.*

White Chocolate Mousse

A delicious variation of the classic favorite. Use good quality chocolate for best results.

Preparation: 30 minutes plus chilling
Yield: 8 servings

8 ounces white chocolate chips
3 tablespoons milk
2 eggs
1 teaspoon vanilla extract
1 cup whipping cream
raspberries for garnish

- Melt chocolate in top of double boiler; stir until smooth.
- Beat milk and eggs with a fork.
- Gradually stir egg mixture into melted chocolate until well blended.
- Cook until slightly thickened, stirring constantly. Do not boil!
- Stir in vanilla, cover and refrigerate 30 minutes.
- Beat whipping cream until soft peaks form.
- Beat chilled chocolate mixture 1 minute on medium speed.
- Gently fold whipped cream into chocolate mixture.
- Spoon into dessert dishes, cover and refrigerate. Serve chilled.
- Garnish with raspberries.

Frangelico Cream

Courtesy of Tippecanoe Place Restaurant, former home of Clement C. Studebaker.

Preparation: 30 minutes
Yield: 8-10 servings

1½ cups superfine sugar
3 egg yolks
1 teaspoon vanilla extract
1½ pounds cream cheese
2 tablespoons Frangelico liqueur
2 cups heavy cream

- Beat sugar, egg yolks and vanilla until light and pale.
- Beat in softened cream cheese; then Frangelico liqueur.
- Set aside in cool place.
- Whip cream until stiff in separate bowl.
- Fold into cheese mixture.
- Pour into goblets and chill.
- Serve plain or with fresh berries or fruit.

Variations: For liqueur cream, replace Frangelico with any fruit brandy or liqueur and garnish with corresponding fruit. For example: Kirsch with cherries, Chambord with raspberries, apricot brandy with apricots.

Brandy Cream

So easy. So good.

Preparation: 20 minutes
Yield: 6 servings

10 scoops vanilla ice cream
1 ounce brandy
1 chocolate covered toffee
** bar, crushed**

- Soften ice cream in mixing bowl.
- Add brandy and whip 3-4 minutes.
- Pour into champagne glasses.
- Garnish with crushed candy.

Variation: Any liqueur can be substituted for the brandy.

Fudge Dip

Dip can also be used as sauce
for cake or ice cream.

Preparation: 25 minutes
Yield: 2 cups

2 cups powdered sugar
1 cup (6 ounces) semi-sweet
** chocolate chips**
½ cup unsalted butter
1 (12 ounce) can evaporated
** milk**
1 teaspoon vanilla extract
¼ cup favorite liqueur
** (optional)**

- In a 2-quart saucepan, combine all ingredients except vanilla and liqueur.
- Cook over medium heat, stirring occasionally, until mixture comes to a full boil (18-20 minutes).
- Boil for 3 minutes, stirring constantly.
- Remove from heat. Stir in vanilla and liqueur.
- Serve with fresh fruit or pound cake.

Caramel Apple Dip

Great for Halloween parties.
Your kids will love it!

Preparation: 10 minutes
Yield: 2 cups

1 (14 ounce) package
** caramels**
2 tablespoons water
1 cup sour cream

- Melt caramels, mixed with water, in double boiler or microwave, stirring occasionally.
- Stir in sour cream.
- Serve with apple slices.

White Chocolate Pear Crème

Courtesy of Herb of Grace Restaurant, located in the Beiger Mansion Inn, Mishawaka, Indiana.

Preparation: 1½ hours plus chilling
Yield: 8-10 servings

Pear Purée

2 cups ripe peeled, cored and chopped pears (3-4 pears)
3 tablespoons butter, melted
⅓ cup sugar
3 tablespoons pear brandy

- Sauté pears in melted butter about 15 minutes.
- Add sugar and stir until pears begin to caramelize, about 10 minutes.
- Pour sautéed pears into workbowl of food processor, add brandy and process until smooth. Set aside.

Crème

10 ounces white chocolate, chopped
¼ cup sweet butter
6 eggs, separated
1 cup powdered sugar
⅓ cup pear brandy
2 cups whipping cream

- Melt white chocolate and butter; set aside.
- In top of double boiler, combine egg yolks, powdered sugar and brandy and beat until mixture falls in ribbons. Continue beating over simmering water 4-5 minutes.
- In large bowl, add egg mixture to the white chocolate mixture.
- Stir until smooth and cool to room temperature.
- Whip cream until quite stiff.
- In a separate bowl, with clean beaters, whip egg whites until stiff.
- Fold egg whites into chocolate mixture and then into the cream.

To serve:
- Spoon crème and pear purée into 8-10 goblets, making 5 layers in each, beginning and ending with crème.
- Chill until set, 2-3 hours.
- Garnish with a leaf painted with white chocolate or mint sprigs.

Flowerpot Pudding

Follow these instructions for a fun children's party or barbecue. For a more elegant dessert, serve layered in a pretty trifle bowl.

Preparation: 40 minutes
Yield: 12 servings

2 cups crushed chocolate sandwich cookies, divided
8 ounces cream cheese, softened
¼ cup margarine, softened
1 cup powdered sugar
2 small (approximately 3¾ ounce) packages instant French vanilla pudding mix
3½ cups milk
12 ounces non-dairy whipped topping

- Place 1 cup crushed cookies in bottom of a clean new 8-inch clay flowerpot.
- Combine cream cheese, margarine and powdered sugar; set aside.
- Prepare pudding according to package directions, using 3½ cups milk.
- Add this to cream cheese mixture and mix well.
- Fold in whipped topping.
- Pour mixture over cookie layer.
- Top with remaining crushed cookies.
- Add artificial flowers to resemble a flowerpot. Serve with a shovel!

Pumpkin Crème Brulée

Courtesy of Flytraps Main Street Bar & Grill, Elkhart, Indiana.

Preparation: 20 minutes
Baking: 1 hour and 10 minutes
Yield: 12 servings

14 egg yolks
1⅓ cups sugar
2 cups pumpkin
1 teaspoon cinnamon
¼ teaspoon allspice
1¼ quarts heavy cream

- Preheat oven to 325°.
- Combine egg yolks and sugar; mix well.
- Add pumpkin, cinnamon and allspice; mix until well blended.
- Heat heavy cream in saucepan until bubbles form around edge of pan.
- Remove from heat and slowly add to pumpkin mixture, stirring constantly.
- Ladle into 12 custard cups. Place cups in large baking pan and fill pan with water until approximately 1 inch deep.
- Bake 1 hour and 10 minutes.
- Remove pan from oven; remove custard cups from water bath. Cool.
- Top with whipped cream, caramel or brown sugar glaze.

Cream Puffs

Cream puffs are very versatile. They may be filled with anything savory or sweet.

Preparation: 20 minutes plus 30 minutes filling and assembly
Baking: 30 minutes
Yield: 30 2-inch cream puffs

Puffs
½ cup butter
1 cup water
1 cup flour
4 eggs

- Preheat oven to 375°.
- In a medium saucepan, bring butter and water to a boil over medium heat.
- Remove from heat. Add flour all at once. Stir well.
- Return to low heat and continue cooking until dough forms a ball and leaves the sides of the pan, about 10 minutes.
- Transfer mixture to a medium mixing bowl. Add eggs one at a time, beating well after each addition.
- On a greased baking sheet, place large rounded tablespoons of the dough 2 inches apart.
- Bake 30 minutes. Cut off the tops and set aside to cool.

Cream Filling
1 cup milk
½ cup sugar
¼ cup flour
2 egg yolks, beaten
2 teaspoons vanilla extract

- In a medium saucepan, heat milk until very hot.
- In a medium bowl, mix sugar and flour. Stir in hot milk. Beat until well blended.
- Transfer mixture back to saucepan. Stir over low heat until very thick and smooth.
- Add egg yolks. Cook 3 minutes.
- Cool, stirring occasionally. Add vanilla.
- Fill cream puffs and replace tops.

Chocolate Frosting
1 cup (6 ounces) semi-sweet or milk chocolate chips
½ cup sour cream

- Melt chocolate chips in the top of a double boiler or in microwave.
- Add sour cream. Stir until well blended.
- Frost cream puffs while icing is still warm.

Peppermint Tea Cookies

A nice after-dinner cookie.

Preparation: 30 minutes plus chilling and assembly
Baking: 8-10 minutes
Yield: 36 2-inch cookies

2 cups sifted flour
1 teaspoon baking powder
½ teaspoon salt
½ cup butter, softened
⅔ cup sugar
1 egg, unbeaten
2 tablespoons light cream
½ teaspoon peppermint extract
6 squares candy-making chocolate
3 tablespoons butter

- Preheat oven to 375°.
- Combine flour, baking powder and salt; sift together.
- Cream ½ cup butter; gradually add sugar and beat until light and fluffy.
- Add egg; beat well.
- Add light cream and peppermint extract.
- Gradually add dry ingredients, blending until smooth.
- Chill 2-3 hours.
- Roll small amounts of dough thin on floured surface.
- Cut with cookie cutter.
- Bake 8-10 minutes on ungreased cookie sheets; let cool.
- Heat chocolate in double boiler until partly melted; remove from heat.
- Add 3 tablespoons butter; stir until chocolate mixture is entirely melted.
- Cool until thickened.
- Spread chocolate on half of the cookies; top with remaining cookies.

Aunt Juanita's Sugar Cookies

Delicate with a shortbread taste.

Preparation: 10 minutes
Baking: 4-6 minutes
Yield: 8 dozen 2-inch cookies

1 cup margarine or butter,
   softened
1 cup vegetable oil
1 cup sugar
1 cup powdered sugar
2 eggs
1½ teaspoons vanilla extract
4 cups flour
1 teaspoon baking soda
1 teaspoon cream of tartar
½ teaspoon salt

- Cream margarine, oil and both sugars.
- Add eggs and vanilla; mix well.
- Sift dry ingredients together; blend into creamed mixture.
- Chill until firm.
- Preheat oven to 400°.
- Roll dough into small balls, using 1 teaspoonful of dough for each.
- Place on lightly greased cookie sheets.
- Flatten with bottom of glass dipped in sugar.
- Bake 4-6 minutes.
- Cool 1 minute on cookie sheet; remove to wire racks to cool completely.

Almond Cookies

One of our favorite cookies.

Preparation: 30 minutes plus chilling
Baking: 20-25 minutes
May be frozen after baking
Yield: 3 to 4 dozen cookies

1 cup butter, softened
1 cup margarine, softened
1 teaspoon almond extract
1½ cups sugar
4 cups cake flour (or
   substitute 4 cups less 2
   tablespoons all-purpose
   flour, plus 2 tablespoons
   cornstarch)
almond slivers

- Cream butter, margarine and almond extract.
- Add sugar and flour.
- Shape into 3 rolls, 1½ inches thick. Wrap in wax paper or plastic wrap.
- Refrigerate one hour.
- Preheat oven to 300°.
- Cut into ½-inch slices; place almond on each slice.
- Bake 20-25 minutes on ungreased cookie sheets.

Easy Cut Sugar Cookies

The secret to this recipe is to cream the butter and sugar thoroughly.

Preparation: 20 minutes plus chilling and frosting
Baking: 8-10 minutes
Freeze well before or after baking
Yield: 3 dozen 3-inch cookies

1 cup butter
1 cup sugar
2 egg yolks (reserve whites for frosting)
1 teaspoon vanilla extract
4 cups flour
1½ teaspoons baking powder
⅓ cup milk

- Cream butter and sugar thoroughly using electric mixer.
- Mix in egg yolks and vanilla.
- Mix in dry ingredients and milk with mixer.
- Chill dough at least 1 hour.
- Preheat oven to 350°.
- Roll out dough, cut out and bake on greased cookie sheets 8-10 minutes.
- Frost when cool.

Frosting
2 egg whites
2½ cups powdered sugar
¼ cup light corn syrup
food coloring

- Beat egg whites until soft peaks form.
- Gradually add powdered sugar, beating until dissolved.
- Add corn syrup; beat one minute.
- Add food coloring as desired.
- Frosting quantity is enough to ice 2 batches of cookies. The frosting can be frozen in plastic container up to 3 months.

Frosted Butter Cookies

Perfect for children and for those who must avoid eggs.

Preparation: 15 minutes
Baking: 8-10 minutes
Yield: 30 cookies

1 cup butter or margarine
½ cup powdered sugar
2 cups plus 2 tablespoons flour
½ teaspoon vanilla extract
½ teaspoon almond extract

- Preheat oven to 375°.
- Cream butter and sugar thoroughly.
- Add flour, vanilla and almond extract; mix well.
- Roll into small balls.
- Place on ungreased cookie sheets, flatten slightly with bottom of glass.
- Bake 8-10 minutes. Cool and frost with Vanilla or Chocolate Frosting.

Vanilla Frosting
3 tablespoons butter
1 cup powdered sugar
2 tablespoons milk
1 teaspoon vanilla extract

- Cream butter and sugar.
- Add milk and vanilla; beat until smooth.
- Frost cookies.

Chocolate Frosting
1 cup powdered sugar
2 tablespoons unsweetened cocoa powder
2 tablespoons hot water
½ teaspoon vanilla extract

- Mix all ingredients together until smooth.
- Frost cookies.

Grandma's Cookies

These are great dunking cookies, the kind your grandmother used to make. Add colored sugar sprinkles for Christmas.

Preparation: 1 ½ hours including frosting
Baking: 10-15 minutes
Yield: 7 dozen cookies

1 teaspoon baking soda
1 cup buttermilk
2 cups sugar
1 cup shortening
2 large or 3 small eggs
3½ cups flour
2 teaspoons baking powder
½ teaspoon salt
2 teaspoons vanilla extract

- Preheat oven to 375°.
- Dissolve baking soda in buttermilk.
- Cream sugar and shortening; add eggs and mix thoroughly.
- Add buttermilk mixture alternately with flour.
- Add baking powder, salt, and vanilla; mix well.
- Drop rounded tablespoonfuls of dough onto ungreased cookie sheets.
- Bake 10-12 minutes.
- Remove immediately from cookie sheets and frost while still hot.

Frosting
4 cups powdered sugar
3 tablespoons margarine
¼ cup milk
1 teaspoon vanilla extract
½ teaspoon lemon juice

- Cream powdered sugar and margarine together.
- Add remaining ingredients and beat until smooth.

Amish Cookies

A true Heartland cookie.

Preparation: 45 minutes plus 2 hours
  chilling
Baking: 12-15 minutes
Yield: 5 dozen 4-inch cookies

5 cups sugar
2½ cups solid shortening
3 eggs
½ cup molasses
1 tablespoon vanilla extract
7 cups flour
2 tablespoons baking soda
2 tablespoons baking powder
1½ teaspoons nutmeg
1 tablespoon cinnamon
1 tablespoon salt
6 cups oatmeal
1 cup buttermilk or sour milk
1 cup raisins
1 cup peanuts, chopped
1 egg white, beaten
2 tablespoons sugar
⅛ teaspoon cinnamon

- Preheat oven to 375°.
- In a very large mixing bowl, combine sugar and shortening. Mix thoroughly.
- Add eggs, molasses, and vanilla. Mix well.
- In a large bowl, sift together flour, baking soda, baking powder, nutmeg, cinnamon, and salt.
- Add the oatmeal to the dry ingredients and mix.
- Add flour mixture gradually to creamed mixture, alternating with the buttermilk.
- Fold in raisins and nuts. Chill 2-3 hours or overnight.
- Using an ice cream scoop, form dough into large balls. Place 4 inches apart on a lightly greased cookie sheet.
- Flatten with fingers. Brush each cookie with beaten egg white. Sprinkle with cinnamon and sugar.
- Bake 12-15 minutes.

White Chocolate Macadamia Nut Cookies

A spectacular combination of flavors!

Preparation: 20 minutes
Baking: 15 minutes
Yield: 4 dozen large cookies

1 pound butter, softened
2 cups sugar
2 cups firmly packed light brown sugar
¼ cup vanilla extract
5 eggs
6 cups flour
2 teaspoons baking soda
1 teaspoon salt
12 ounces white chocolate chunks
3½ ounces macadamia nuts, coarsely chopped

- Preheat oven to 325°.
- In a very large bowl, beat together butter and sugars until light and creamy.
- Beat in vanilla and eggs until smooth.
- Combine flour, soda and salt.
- Gradually beat the flour mixture into the butter mixture.
- Mix in chocolate chunks and nuts; batter will be very stiff.
- Using a small ice cream scoop or ¼-cup measure, drop batter onto greased cookie sheets, placing 3 inches apart to allow for spreading.
- Bake 15 minutes or until light golden brown.
- Let cool on cookie sheet before removing to a wire rack.

Cornucopia Carob Chip Cookies

Courtesy of Cornucopia Restaurant, South Bend, Indiana.

Preparation: 1 hour
Baking: 12 minutes
Yield: 4 dozen cookies

1 cup butter, softened
1⅓ cups honey
1 egg
½ teaspoon salt
2 teaspoons vanilla extract
1 teaspoon baking powder
4 cups whole wheat flour
⅓ cup milk powder
1⅓ cups carob chips

- Preheat oven to 350°.
- Cream butter and honey.
- Add egg, salt and vanilla.
- In separate bowl, mix dry ingredients. Add to honey butter.
- Add carob chips and mix well.
- Drop by rounded teaspoonfuls onto greased cookie sheet.
- Bake 12 minutes; remove to wire racks and cool.

Big and Luscious Chocolate Chip Cookies

The ultimate chocolate chip cookie!

Preparation: 15 minutes
Baking: 10-12 minutes
Yield: 7½-8 dozen huge cookies

1 pound butter (no substitutes)
1½ cups sugar
2 cups firmly packed dark brown sugar
3 eggs
2 teaspoons vanilla extract
5 cups flour
1½ teaspoons baking soda
1½ teaspoons salt
1 cup oatmeal
4 cups (24 ounces) chocolate chips
1 cup chopped pecans

- Preheat oven to 350°.
- Cream butter and both sugars well.
- Add eggs and vanilla; mix well.
- Combine flour, baking soda and salt; add to creamed mixture. This may be hard to mix; mixing with clean hands works well.
- Stir in oatmeal, chocolate chips and nuts.
- Drop dough by rounded tablespoonfuls onto ungreased cookie sheets; dough should be size of golf balls. Flatten slightly.
- Bake 10-12 minutes.

Variation: 2 cups butterscotch chips may be substituted for 2 cups of chocolate chips.

Forgotten Cookies

Popular cookie for holiday cookie exchange.

Preparation: 15 minutes plus 6 hours standing time
Yield: 24 cookies

2 egg whites
⅔ cup sugar
1 teaspoon vanilla extract
1 cup chopped pecans
1 cup mini-chocolate chips

- Preheat oven to 350°.
- Beat egg whites until stiff.
- Gradually add sugar and beat until stiff.
- Add vanilla, pecans and chocolate chips, and stir gently.
- Drop by teaspoonfuls onto foil-covered cookie sheets.
- Place in oven and then turn it off.
- Leave in oven at least 6 hours or overnight.

Variation: 1 cup crushed chocolate toffee bars (about 4 candy bars) or 1 cup butterscotch chips may be substituted for the chocolate chips.

Chocolate Cookies

Soft inside, crisp outside.

Preparation: 15 minutes
Baking: 8-9 minutes
Yield: 4 to 5 dozen

1¼ cups butter, softened
2 cups sugar
2 eggs
2 teaspoons vanilla extract
2 cups flour
¾ cup unsweetened cocoa
   powder
1 teaspoon baking soda
½ teaspoon salt

- Preheat oven to 350°.
- Cream butter and sugar in large bowl.
- Add eggs and vanilla; blend well.
- Combine all dry ingredients.
- Blend into creamed mixture.
- Drop by teaspoonfuls, 3 inches apart, onto ungreased cookie sheets.
- Bake 8-9 minutes.
- Cool one minute on cookie sheet to set; cool completely on wire rack.

Apricot Triangles

An excellent crust as well as a tasty filling.

Preparation: 1 hour plus chilling time
Baking: 12 minutes
Yield: 3 to 4 dozen cookies

1 cup margarine, softened
8 ounces cream cheese,
   softened
2 cups sifted flour
1¾ cups dried apricots
½ cup firmly packed brown
   sugar
1 cup cut-up dates
2 tablespoons water
1 cup finely chopped nuts

- Cream margarine and cream cheese.
- Add flour; blend well.
- Wrap dough in wax paper or plastic wrap and refrigerate several hours or overnight.
- Preheat oven to 350°.
- Place apricots and brown sugar in workbowl of food processor; process until finely chopped.
- In a medium saucepan, combine apricots and brown sugar with dates and water; cook 3 minutes.
- Add chopped nuts.
- Roll dough very thin; cut into 3-inch squares.
- Place one tablespoon filling on each square; fold over to form triangle.
- Pinch edges together.
- Bake 12 minutes; remove from oven and cool on wire rack.

German Chocolate Cake Cookies

Time consuming, but well worth the effort.

Preparation: 1 ½ hours
Baking: 12-14 minutes
Freezes well
Yield: 4 dozen

Dough

4 cups flour
¼ cup unsweetened cocoa powder
1 teaspoon salt
2 cups powdered sugar
2 cups margarine, softened
4 teaspoons vanilla extract

- Preheat oven to 350°.
- In a medium bowl, sift together flour, cocoa, and salt.
- In a large bowl, cream powdered sugar, margarine, and vanilla until light and fluffy.
- Blend flour mixture into margarine mixture. Mix well. Dough will be stiff.
- Using 2 tablespoons of dough, form into balls. Place on ungreased cookie sheets 2 inches apart. Make an indentation in each cookie with your finger.
- Bake for 12-14 minutes or until slightly brown around edges.

Filling

⅔ cup evaporated milk
⅔ cup sugar
2 egg yolks, beaten
⅓ cup margarine
1 teaspoon vanilla extract
¾ cup chopped pecans
1¼ cups shredded coconut

- In a medium saucepan, combine milk, sugar, egg yolks, margarine, and vanilla.
- Cook over medium heat, stirring constantly, 5-8 minutes or until mixture is slightly thick and gold in color.
- Remove from heat. Mixture will get slightly thicker as it cools.
- Add pecans and coconut.
- Let cool 15-20 minutes.
- Drop small amount of filling into indentation in each cookie.

Topping

½ cup milk chocolate chips
2 tablespoons water
2 tablespoons margarine
½ cup sifted powdered sugar

- In a small saucepan, combine chocolate chips, water and margarine.
- Cook over low heat, stirring constantly, until smooth.
- Add powdered sugar; stir until smooth.
- Drizzle topping over each cookie.
- Store in airtight tins or freeze.

French Waffle Cookies

A delicate little cookie.
Delicious served with jam for
afternoon tea.

Preparation: 10 minutes
Baking: 2-7 minutes
Yield: 10 dozen cookies

12 egg yolks
1 pound margarine, softened
2½ cups sugar
4 cups flour
2 teaspoons vanilla extract
8 egg whites
powdered sugar

- Combine egg yolks, margarine, sugar, flour and vanilla; mix well.
- Beat egg whites until stiff.
- Fold gently into flour mixture.
- Drop by teaspoonfuls onto hot waffle iron.
- When light brown, remove and dust with powdered sugar.

Pecan Tarts

Freezes well after baking.

Preparation: 30 minutes
Baking: 13-15 minutes
Yield: 36 tarts

Shells
½ cup margarine
½ cup sugar
2 egg yolks
1 teaspoon vanilla or almond
**   extract**
2 cups flour

- Preheat oven to 400°.
- Cream margarine and sugar together.
- Add egg yolks, extract and flour; beat until crumbly.
- Place 1 heaping teaspoonful of dough into mini-muffin pan; press around edge to make crust.
- Bake 8-10 minutes; fill while still hot.

Filling
½ cup margarine
⅓ cup dark corn syrup
1 cup powdered sugar
1 cup chopped pecans
18 whole pecans, cut in half

- Decrease oven to 350°.
- Combine margarine, dark corn syrup and powdered sugar in small saucepan; bring to a boil.
- Add chopped pecans.
- Spoon into hot shells.
- Top with pecan half.
- Bake 5 minutes.
- Cool; remove from pan carefully with sharp knife.

Kieflies

A much requested recipe from our first cookbook, Nutbread and Nostalgia.

Preparation: 1 ½ hours plus chilling
Baking: 12 minutes
Yield: 6 dozen cookies

Cookie
6 cups flour
1½ teaspoons salt
2 cups butter
12 egg yolks, whites reserved
1 cup sour cream
1 teaspoon vanilla extract

- Mix flour and salt together.
- Cut butter into flour mixture until completely blended.
- In a separate bowl, mix egg yolks, sour cream and vanilla. Add to flour and butter mixture.
- Blend and knead until mixture is consistency of pie dough.
- Form into small walnut size balls.
- Refrigerate overnight.

Filling
12 egg whites
3½ cups powdered sugar
6 cups (about 1½ pounds) chopped nuts

- Beat egg whites until stiff but not dry.
- Add sugar and mix well.
- Stir in nuts by hand.
- Refrigerate until ready to use.

To assemble:
- Preheat oven to 350°.
- Take a few balls from the refrigerator. Roll each ball into a thin circle on well-floured surface.
- Place a heaping teaspoonful of filling on each circle.
- Roll up into crescent shape and pinch ends.
- Bake 12 minutes.
- Cool and sprinkle with powdered sugar.

Raspberry Brownies

These look best the day they're made, but taste great as long as they last!

Preparation: 20 minutes
Baking: 30 minutes
Yield: 24 brownies

1 cup butter or margarine, softened
1¼ cups sugar
½ cup firmly packed light brown sugar
4 eggs
⅔ cup unsweetened cocoa powder
1½ teaspoons vanilla extract
1¼ cups flour
½ pint fresh raspberries
powdered sugar

- Preheat oven to 350°.
- Beat butter and both sugars together until fluffy.
- Add eggs, one at a time, beating well after each addition.
- Stir in cocoa and vanilla.
- Gently mix in flour.
- Pour batter into greased 9x13-inch baking pan. Sprinkle raspberries over batter.
- Bake 30 minutes or until brownies test done.
- Cool in pan on wire rack.
- Sprinkle with powdered sugar.
- Cut into 24 brownies.
- Store at room temperature.

Peanut Butter Diamonds

Unbelievably easy...unbelievably delicious!

Preparation: 15 minutes plus chilling
Yield: 20-25 bars

2 cups graham cracker crumbs
4 cups powdered sugar
1½ cups margarine, divided
2 cups creamy peanut butter
2 cups (12 ounces) chocolate chips

- Combine graham cracker crumbs and sugar.
- Melt 1 cup margarine; mix with peanut butter.
- Add to crumb mixture.
- Press into bottom of 15x10x1-inch jelly roll pan.
- Melt chocolate chips and ½ cup margarine.
- Pour over crust.
- Refrigerate 5 minutes and cut into bars.

Chocolate Mousse Brownies

The best brownie ever made!

Preparation: 30 minutes
Baking: 40 minutes
Yield: 35 brownies

Brownie Layer

½ cup margarine
2 cups (12 ounces) chocolate
   chips
1⅔ cups sugar
1¼ cups flour
1 teaspoon vanilla extract
½ teaspoon baking powder
½ teaspoon salt
3 eggs
1 cup chopped nuts
   (optional)

- Preheat oven to 350°.
- Melt margarine and chocolate chips over low heat, stirring constantly.
- Stir in remaining ingredients, except nuts; mix until smooth.
- Add nuts; spread into greased 9x13-inch baking pan.

Mousse Topping

¾ cup whipping cream
1 cup (6 ounces) chocolate
   chips
3 eggs
⅓ cup sugar
⅛ teaspoon salt

- Heat cream and chocolate chips over low heat, stirring constantly, until melted and smooth. Cool slightly.
- Combine remaining ingredients and beat until foamy.
- Stir into chocolate mixture.
- Pour topping evenly over batter.
- Bake 40 minutes; cool 2 hours before cutting into squares.

Raspberry Chocolate Bars

Fabulous! Serve as often as possible!

Preparation:1 hour plus cooling time
Baking: 25 minutes
Yield: 40 bars

Base
4 ounces unsweetened chocolate
½ cup butter
2 cups sugar
¼ teaspoon salt
1 teaspoon vanilla extract
4 eggs
1 cup flour

- Preheat oven to 350°.
- Melt chocolate and butter over low heat; cool.
- Combine remaining ingredients; beat thoroughly.
- Stir in chocolate mixture just until blended.
- Spread into greased 9x13-inch baking pan.
- Bake 25 minutes or until set.
- Cool 30 minutes.

Filling
½ cup seedless raspberry preserves
2 ounces semi-sweet chocolate
1 ounce unsweetened chocolate
⅓ cup sugar
¼ cup water
2 eggs
1 cup butter, softened

- Spread preserves over cooled base.
- Melt chocolates together over low heat; let cool.
- Bring sugar and water to a boil; boil one minute.
- Beat eggs until frothy in large bowl.
- Gradually add sugar-water mixture to eggs; beat on high speed for 5 minutes.
- Gradually add butter, ½ tablespoon at a time, beating well after each addition. Mixture may appear curdled.
- Add melted chocolate; beat until smooth.
- Spread carefully over preserves.

Chocolate Glaze
1 ounce unsweetened chocolate
1 tablespoon butter

- Melt chocolate and butter together over low heat, stirring until smooth.
- Drizzle over filling.
- Refrigerate one hour; cut into bars.

Rocky Road Fudge Bars

These are absolutely wonderful!

Preparation: 45 minutes
Baking: 27-37 minutes
Yield: 40 bars

Bar

½ cup margarine
1 ounce unsweetened
  chocolate
1 cup sugar
1 cup flour
½-1 cup chopped walnuts
1 teaspoon vanilla extract
2 eggs

- Preheat oven to 350°.
- Grease and flour 9x13-inch baking pan.
- Melt margarine and chocolate over low heat.
- Add remaining ingredients and mix well.
- Spread into prepared pan.

Filling

6 ounces cream cheese,
  softened
½ cup sugar
2 tablespoons flour
¼ cup margarine, softened
1 egg
½ teaspoon vanilla extract
¼ cup chopped walnuts
1 cup (6 ounces) chocolate
  chips
2 cups mini-marshmallows

- Combine cream cheese with sugar, flour, margarine, egg and vanilla.
- Beat 1 minute until smooth and fluffy.
- Stir in nuts; spread over bar mixture.
- Sprinkle with chocolate chips.
- Bake 25-35 minutes; remove from oven.
- Sprinkle with marshmallows; bake 2 minutes longer.

Frosting

¼ cup margarine
1 ounce unsweetened
  chocolate
2 ounces cream cheese
¼ cup milk
3 cups powdered sugar
1 teaspoon vanilla extract

- Melt margarine, chocolate, cream cheese and milk over low heat.
- Stir in powdered sugar and vanilla until smooth.
- Immediately pour over marshmallows and swirl with a knife.
- Cool; cut into bars. Store in refrigerator.

Butter Chews

They melt in your mouth!

Preparation: 15 minutes
Baking: 40 minutes
Yield: 40 squares

Crust
¾ cup butter
1½ cups flour
3 tablespoons sugar

- Preheat oven to 375°.
- Mix butter, flour and sugar.
- Pat into greased 9x13-inch baking pan.
- Bake 15 minutes.

Filling
3 eggs, separated
2¼ cups firmly packed brown
**   sugar**
¾ cup coconut
1 cup chopped pecans
powdered sugar

- Beat egg yolks.
- Add brown sugar, coconut and pecans.
- Beat egg whites until stiff.
- Fold beaten egg whites into brown sugar mixture.
- Spread over baked crust.
- Bake 25-30 minutes.
- Remove from oven and dust with powdered sugar.
- Cool; cut into bars.

Mixed Nut Bars

Rich and nutty.

Preparation: 20 minutes
Baking: 20 minutes
Freezes very well
Yield: 40 small bars

Crust
½ cup butter, softened
¼ cup sugar
½ cup firmly packed brown
**   sugar**
1½ cups flour
12 ounces mixed salted nuts

- Preheat oven to 350°.
- Cream butter and both sugars together.
- Add flour and mix well.
- Press into 9x13-inch baking pan.
- Bake 10 minutes; remove from oven.
- Pour nuts over crust.

Butterscotch Sauce
1 cup (6 ounces) butterscotch
**   chips**
½ cup white corn syrup
2 tablespoons butter
1 tablespoon water

- Melt all ingredients in double boiler.
- Pour melted mixture over nuts.
- Bake additional 10 minutes.
- Cut while still warm into small squares.

Pecan Squares

Rich and delicious!

Preparation: 15 minutes
Baking: 35-40 minutes
Freezes well after cut
Yield: 16 to 25 squares

Crust
1⅓ cups flour
2 tablespoons firmly packed brown sugar
½ cup butter or margarine, softened

- Preheat oven to 350°.
- Blend crust ingredients thoroughly.
- Press mixture firmly into bottom of greased 9-inch square baking pan.
- Bake 15 minutes.

Pecan Filling
2 eggs, slightly beaten
½ cup light corn syrup
½ cup firmly packed brown sugar
2 tablespoons margarine, melted
1 teaspoon vanilla extract
¾ cup chopped pecans

- Combine filling ingredients.
- Pour over baked crust.
- Return to oven for 20-25 minutes or until center is firm.
- Cool and cut into squares.

Chess Squares

Very rich!

Preparation: 15 minutes
Baking: 45 minutes
Yield: 36-40 small squares

1 box yellow butter recipe cake mix
½ cup butter, melted
3 eggs
8 ounces cream cheese, softened
1 teaspoon vanilla extract
4 cups powdered sugar

- Preheat oven to 325°.
- Stir together cake mix, butter and 1 egg by hand.
- Press into greased 9x13-inch baking pan.
- Combine remaining 2 eggs, cream cheese, vanilla and powdered sugar; mix thoroughly.
- Pour over crust; bake 45 minutes.
- Cut into squares when cool.

Chocolate Cinnamon Shortbread

A "not-so-sweet" sweet. Great with your morning cup of coffee!

Preparation: 10 minutes
Baking: 25 minutes
Yield: 32 wedges

2 cups flour, sifted
¼ cup unsweetened cocoa
   powder
¾ cup powdered sugar
½ teaspoon cinnamon
1 cup cold unsalted butter
1 tablespoon sugar
⅛ teaspoon cinnamon

- Preheat oven to 350°.
- Combine flour, cocoa, powdered sugar and ½ teaspoon cinnamon in workbowl of food processor. Pulse to mix.
- Slice butter into flour mixture.
- Pulse until butter is completely blended in and mixture resembles fine meal. Mixture should stick together when pressed between thumb and forefinger.
- Divide dough in half; press each half into ungreased 8-inch cake pan.
- Combine 1 tablespoon sugar and ⅛ teaspoon cinnamon.
- Sprinkle shortbread with cinnamon-sugar mixture.
- Bake 10 minutes.
- Remove from oven; prick entire surface with a fork.
- Return pans to oven and bake additional 15 minutes.
- Cool and cut each shortbread into 16 wedges.
- Serve with coffee or vanilla ice cream.

Cheesecake Bars

Nice flavor—wonderful for a ladies' luncheon. This recipe can be doubled and baked in a 9x13-inch baking pan.

Preparation: 15 minutes
Baking: 40 minutes
Yield: 32 bars

5 tablespoons butter or margarine
⅓ cup firmly packed brown sugar
1 cup flour
½ cup chopped nuts
½ cup sugar
8 ounces cream cheese, softened
1 egg
2 tablespoons milk
1 tablespoon lemon juice
¼ teaspoon vanilla extract

- Preheat oven to 350°.
- Cream butter and brown sugar.
- Add flour and nuts; mix well.
- Set aside 1 cup of nut mixture for topping.
- Press remainder in bottom of 8-inch square baking pan.
- Bake 12-15 minutes.
- Blend sugar and cream cheese until smooth.
- Add egg, milk, lemon juice and vanilla; beat well.
- Spread over crust.
- Sprinkle with reserved 1 cup topping.
- Return to oven; bake an additional 25 minutes.
- Cool and chill; cut into triangles or squares.

Apricot Bars

Strawberry or raspberry jam may be substituted for apricot jam.

Preparation: 15 minutes
Baking: 30-35 minutes
Yield: 40-48 bars

1 cup sugar
1 cup butter, softened
2 egg yolks
2 cups flour
1 tablespoon vanilla extract
10 ounces apricot jam

- Preheat oven to 350°.
- Combine all ingredients except jam; mix with pastry blender until mixture forms a soft dough.
- Reserve ¾ cup dough for topping.
- Press remaining dough into bottom of 9x13-inch baking pan.
- Spread with jam.
- Break off small pieces of remaining dough. Flatten and place on top of jam.
- Bake 30-35 minutes. Cool and cut into bars.

Simple Fudge

An old family favorite that is easy to make.

3 ounces unsweetened chocolate
¼ cup butter or margarine
3 cups powdered sugar, sifted
1 egg
2 teaspoons vanilla extract
1 cup chopped pecans (optional)

Preparation: 20 minutes plus chilling
Yield: 64 candies

- Line an 8-inch square pan with wax paper.
- Melt chocolate and margarine in saucepan over low heat.
- Add 1½ cups powdered sugar to chocolate mixture, stirring until well blended.
- Beat in egg and vanilla.
- Add remaining 1½ cups powdered sugar and stir until smooth.
- Add pecans, if desired.
- Press fudge into prepared pan. Chill until firm.
- Cut into squares.

Peanut Butter Fudge

Try topping this with Simple Fudge—yummy!

2 cups sugar
⅔ cup evaporated milk
1 cup marshmallow creme
1 cup peanut butter
1 tablespoon vanilla extract

Preparation: 30 minutes plus cooling
Yield: 36 candies

- Line a 9-inch square pan with wax paper.
- Combine sugar and milk in saucepan.
- Boil, stirring occasionally, until mixture reaches soft ball stage (240° on candy thermometer).
- Remove from heat and stir in marshmallow creme, peanut butter and vanilla.
- Pour peanut butter mixture into prepared pan. Cool.
- To cut, invert pan onto cutting board. Remove wax paper and cut into 36 pieces.

Rum Balls

*Servings not too big but potent.
Not for the kids!*

*Preparation: 1½ hours plus 3 days
   setting time
Freezes well
Yield: 5 dozen candies*

3 cups crushed vanilla wafers
1 cup sifted powdered sugar
**3 tablespoons unsweetened
   cocoa powder**
¼ teaspoon salt
**1½ cups finely chopped
   pecans or walnuts**
¼ cup brandy
¼ cup rum
powdered sugar for rolling

- Combine all ingredients except powdered sugar for rolling.
- Roll into small balls, ¾-inch to 1-inch in diameter.
- Let stand 30 minutes.
- Roll in powdered sugar.
- Store in airtight container for 3 days before serving.

*Variation: ¼ cup coffee-flavored liqueur and ⅓ cup hazelnut
or other liqueur may be substituted for brandy and rum.*

Chocolate Cream Truffles

*These are pretty when served in
small foil cups.*

*Preparation: 30 minutes
Yield: 2½ dozen candies*

**2 cups (12 ounces) chocolate
   chips**
¼ cup sour cream
**2 tablespoons almond-
   flavored liqueur**
**⅔ cup finely chopped toasted
   almonds**

- Melt chocolate chips in double boiler over hot, not boiling, water.
- Stir until smooth and remove from heat.
- Blend in sour cream and liqueur; mix well.
- Chill until firm enough to shape into balls.
- Drop balls onto wax paper-lined baking sheet.
- Roll in almonds until evenly coated.
- Chill until firm.

Maple Cinnamon Pecans

*Place around the room in those
fancy little silver bowls you
never get to use!*

*Preparation: 1 ¼ hours
Yield: 1 pound pecans*

1 egg white
½ teaspoon cold water
½ teaspoon maple flavoring
1 pound pecan halves
½ cup sugar
¼ teaspoon salt
½ teaspoon cinnamon

- Preheat oven to 225°.
- Beat egg white, water and maple flavoring until frothy, not stiff.
- Add nuts and stir gently until coated.
- Add sugar, salt and cinnamon. Mix well.
- Place in buttered jelly roll pan.
- Bake 1 hour, stirring every 15 minutes.

Sugar and Spice Pecans

*Delicious snack for cocktail
parties.*

*Preparation: 10 minutes
Yield: 2 cups pecans*

2 teaspoons butter, melted
**¼ cup firmly packed brown
   sugar**
½ teaspoon cinnamon
¼ teaspoon salt
¼ teaspoon nutmeg
⅛ teaspoon orange extract
1 tablespoon water
2 cups pecans

- Combine all ingredients except pecans in a 1-quart glass bowl; mix well.
- Add pecans and stir to coat well.
- Place in microwave for 5 minutes, stirring after each minute with a wooden spoon.
- Cool on wax paper separating each nut.

Mini Chocolate Cups

Chocolate lover's delight.

Preparation: 45 minutes plus chilling
Yield: 24 servings

Cups
**2 cups (12 ounces) chocolate
chips**
2 tablespoons butter

- Melt chocolate chips with butter in top of double boiler.
- Spread mixture on bottom and sides of 24 mini cupcake tins.
- Freeze 1 hour.
- To remove from tins: let chocolate-lined tins sit at room temperature for 1 minute. Scrape edges of cups with a sharp knife. They will pop out.

Chocolate Mousse Filling
3 eggs, separated
1 cup heavy cream, whipped
**1 cup (6 ounces) chocolate
chips, melted**
1 teaspoon rum or brandy
**whipped cream, nuts, or
cherries for garnish**

- In a medium bowl, beat egg whites until stiff. Set aside.
- In a separate bowl, combine whipped cream, egg yolks, melted chocolate, and rum or brandy.
- Fold in beaten egg whites.
- Spoon into chocolate cups. Garnish with whipped cream or nuts or cherries.

Peanut Butter Cups

Better than store bought!

Preparation: 40 minutes
Yield: 32-36 candies

¼ cup butter
**¾ cup graham cracker
crumbs**
¾ cup powdered sugar
**¾ cup chunky or smooth
peanut butter**
**1 cup (6 ounces) chocolate
chips**

- Melt butter in microwave.
- Stir in graham cracker crumbs, powdered sugar and peanut butter until smooth.
- Line miniature cupcake tins with paper liners.
- Fill each cup ¾ full with mixture.
- Pat mixture into cups until top is smooth.
- Melt chocolate chips and spread over the peanut butter mixture. Do not make chocolate layer too thick.
- Refrigerate up to 2 weeks.

213

Chocolate-Dipped Strawberries

Simple, understated elegance.

Preparation: 20 minutes plus setting time
Yield: 12 strawberries

1 cup (6 ounces) milk chocolate chips
1 tablespoon shortening
1 pint large strawberries, washed, dried and chilled

- Melt chocolate chips and shortening in top of double boiler over hot, not boiling, water.
- Stir until smooth.
- Hold each strawberry by the stem and dip ¾ of the way into the chocolate.
- Place dipped strawberries on wax paper-lined baking sheet.
- Allow to harden approximately 30 minutes before serving.
- These may be refrigerated up to 4 hours before serving.

Acknowledgments

The Junior League of South Bend, Indiana, wishes to acknowledge those who have been invaluable with their assistance in the creation of **Great Beginnings, Grand Finales**. Our gratitude is immeasurable.

Marcia Adams
Beiger Mansion Inn
Peggy Beyler
Peggy Bolka
Tim and Tammy Ciszczon
Dan Daniels
Design Ink, Inc.
Tom Devoe
Karen Faulkner
Sue Fredericks
Granger Graphics, Inc.
John Hoban
Kroger Co.

Jeff Leonard
John Lloyd
Miami Florist & Gift Shoppe
Northern Indiana Historical Society, Inc.
University of Notre Dame
Ruthmere House Museum
Selmer Company, LP
Paula Sipotz
Tabor Hill Winery
Margaret Thomas
Wygant Floral Company, Inc.
Kathy Zehnder

We would also like to express our gratitude to all our sister Leagues who shared all their experiences and advice with us. The success of this book is due entirely to the wonderful members, families, and friends of our Junior League who contributed their favorite recipes, tested them and tasted them. It is our sincere hope that no one has been inadvertently omitted.

Diane Albright
Roberta Alfrey
Jean Axelberg
Beth Axelberg
Mary Jane Bagatini
Carol Baker
Nancy Ball
Nancy Baranay
Pat Bayliss
Mary Jo Beardsley
Kathi Benedix
Lillian Bird
Kathy Bishop
Laurie Blanchard
Louise Blanchard
JoAnn Blazek
Lona Bradford
Linda Brady
Noreen Busch

Kathy Bussmann
Maureen Cahir
Maureen Calier
Peggy Carberry
Lynn Cassady
Jean Charles
Sue Cholis
Ritie Clemency
Linda Clements
Suzanne Coffey
Adrienne Cohoat
Diane Coiro
Louise Corpora
Pat Costigan
Alene Culver
Karen Curtis
Judy Decker
Katy Demarais
Angie Dennig

Lynne Donoho
Wendy Drost
Joyce Dunfee
Paula Eide
Jane Emanoil
Julie Englert
Madeline Ettl
Norvella Farabaugh
Laura Flynn
Charlotte Ford
Trish Ford
Jennifer Fox Brooks
Kari Frankenberg
Becky Freehauf
Donna Freidline
Joan Frieling
Krista Furry
Jan Gates
Marion Gauthier

Jackie Gearhart
Theckla Gerstbauer
Margaret Gerstbauer
Pam Gibboney
Priscilla Glueckert
Debbi Gobdel
Nancy Goodhew
Sherri Goodwin
Diane Gorman
Linda Grainger
Marion Green
Barb Green
Linda Griffin
Susan Gustafson
Carolyn Hahn
Shirley Hamilton
Judy Hansen
Joan Hardig
Bonnie Hay
Sandra Hayes
Laurey Henry
Kathy Hickey
Anne Hillauer
Jill Hillman
Monica Hoban
Karen Hollis
Janice Horan
Jean James
Pam Jarrett
Becky Jellison
Cindy Joers
Mary Johnson
Lois Jones
Leslie Jones
Marijo Kelly
Peggy King
Genelle King
Jo Knoop
Shirlee Korte
Karen Kroft
Lynn Kuehn
Christine Kuntz
Patti Kuroski
Donna Kyle
Lisa Laakso
Linda Laskowski
Judith Lentych
Ann Lindsey
Debbie Locsi
Barb Lorch
Debbie Luther
Jan Lutz

Jeri Maceika
Margo MacGregor
Sally Mager
Joan Mansfield
Pam Matz
Jan Matz
Joyce McFadden
Anne McGraw
Kathy McLaughlin
Roberta McMahon
JoJo Meehan
Norma Meehan
Cindy Merrett
Marilyn Metros
Jane Metz
Emee Miller
Susan Morton
Martha Moynahan
Pam Mullin
Kate Murphy
Cindy Murphy
Jane Murphy
Teddi Murray
Barbara Nawrot
Sharon Nelson
Joan New
Ilene New
Pam Newman
Joan Noble
Mary Pat Nussbaum
Pat Odlag
Elinor Olson
Jennifer Osthimer
Mary Pajakowski
Diana Panzica
Terese Partyka
Leslie Paul
Myrna Perkins
Mary Peterson
Charlene Pippenger
Cinda Pittman
Jeri Powell
Linda Racine
Mary Reineke
MaryAnn Rogers
Ina Rosenberg
Jill Ross
Trish Ross
Jennifer Rousos
Sue Ruszkowski
Debbie Rykovich
Sue Schlifke

Tamara Schneider
Sarah Schroeder
Cheri Schuster
Kathy Seidl
Bonnie Shaffer
Susan Shetterly
Susan Shields
Sue Shirrell
Jeanette Simon
Judy Simpson
Diana Skogsbergh
Cathy Sompels
Barb Sorensen
Becky Sramek
Mary Sterrenberg
Jolene Stiver
Sandra Stone
Candice Stoner
Sandra Stoner
Robyn Menna Strausser
Teresa Swartzbaugh
Christy Szarwark
Pam Szmanda
Margaret Thomas
Janet Thompson
Judy Trierweiler
Holly Troeger
Dionn Tron
Posi Tucker
Nancy Turner
Theresa Tyler
Nancy Tyler
Sally Walker
Diane Walters
Margaret Walz
Marcia Warter
Nancy Wasson
Dottie Webster
Lisa Weisser
Roberta Westerfield
Roberta Westfall
Barb Whalen
Joyce Wilhelm
Suzie Wilkinson
Marsha Williams
Marjie Witsken
Mary Woodham
Jane Wright
Ruthie Wurzburg
Diane Young
Betsy Zima

INDEX

Junior League of South Bend, Inc.

P.O. Box 1452
South Bend, IN 46624
219 / 258-6071

Please send me:	Price	Quantity	Total
Nutbread and Nostalgia	$16.95	_____	$ _____
Great Beginnings, Grand Finales	$18.95	_____	$ _____
SUBTOTAL			$ _____
Indiana residents add 5% sales tax			$ _____
Shipping at $3.00 each, or $5.00 for both			$ _____
TOTAL ENCLOSED			$ _____

SEND TO:

Name_____

Address_____

City_____State _____ Zip_____

Gift From _____

Please make checks payable to **Junior League of South Bend, Inc.**

Please do not send cash. Sorry, no C.O.D.'s.

Please charge my ☐ VISA ☐ MasterCard

Card Number_____ Expiration Date_____

Cardholder's Signature _____

Telephone credit card purchases are welcome.

*Profits from the sale of these cookbooks are used to support the many
community projects of the Junior League of South Bend, Inc.*

I would like to see **Great Beginnings, Grand Finales** in the the following stores:

Store Name _____

Address _____

City _____ State _____ Zip _____

Store Name _____

Address _____

City _____ State _____ Zip _____

Store Name _____

Address _____

City _____ State _____ Zip _____

Store Name _____

Address _____

City _____ State _____ Zip _____

Store Name _____

Address _____

City _____ State _____ Zip _____

Store Name _____

Address _____

City _____ State _____ Zip _____

Thank You!